Our Mothers Ourselves

Six women from across the world tell their mothers' stories

CATHY HULL

RUPAL SHAH

CARYN SOLOMON

VEENA SIDDHARTH

KUMI KONNO

VAYU NAIDU

AUSTIN MACAULEY PUBLISHERS™

LONDON • CAMBRIDGE • NEW YORK • SHARJAH

A CIP catalogue record for this title is available from the British Library.

ISBN 9781398449848 (Paperback)
ISBN 9781398449862 (ePub e-book)
ISBN 9781398449855 (Audiobook)

www.austinmacauley.com

First Published 2022
Austin Macauley Publishers Ltd
1 Canada Square
Canary Wharf
London
E14 5AA

DEDICATIONS

We would like to thank one another for the trust and friendship that allowed these stories to coalesce; and to thank our mothers Audie, Sarla, Joan, Saroja, Sadako and Jayarukmini for sharing their stories and for all the rest.

CONTENTS

FOREWORD

From the earliest times, as humans, we have tried to capture the spirit of people who have gone before, through stories, art and music. Our awareness that we walk in the footsteps of those who came before us is a fundamental part of the human story. Since time immemorial, as we grapple with meaning, we have yearned to understand how we are shaped by our ancestors.

Nevertheless, most of us will be lost to history, forgotten by our descendants; and our stories, struggles and triumphs will die with us. In this book, we set out to honour those with whom we've shared a body, a name, a home, a childhood and countless memories – those without whom we would not be who we are now. By telling their stories as we know them, we bring them back and introduce them to those who follow.

Here, we tell the lives of our mothers, all of them 'ordinary women', but each in her own way extraordinary and heroic, who taught their daughters how to live. Their stories span four continents and were shaped by some of the major events that took place in the twentieth century, including World Wars One and Two, colonialism and the ending of Apartheid in South Africa.

The idea for the book grew out of sharing our own stories of growing up and realising that although we thought we understood our mothers' lives, we didn't know enough. Some of us wanted simply to hear what our mothers had never told us. Others wanted to explore what our mothers handed down and how this influenced our own mothering.

These six stories reflect the different times, places, class, social context sand cultures in which our mothers lived out their lives. They speak of western, individualistic ideas of mothering as well as eastern, mythological understandings of the 'universal mother' embodied in us all.

But despite their differences, the women described in this anthology share an 'essence' – they all dared to be different. The Second World War offered Cathy's mother the chance to escape her restricted family background in northern England, to forge a new life for herself in the south. Kumi's mother moved to the southernmost part of the mainland to live with adoptive parents in her childhood and later went to Tokyo, not far from her birthplace, to study at university. Vayu's mother was among the first generation of Indian women to have access to higher education and ended up mobilising the supply of milk to soldiers and refugee wives and children to give them much-needed calcium in their diet; an insufficiency she herself had known during World War Two. Caryn's mother was deeply involved in the anti-apartheid movement in South Africa, putting her own life at risk as well as the lives of her family. The colonial ties between India and the UK enabled Rupal's mother to take the unprecedented step of migrating to London to marry a man she hadn't seen for five years; while Veena's mother left India as a single woman, hoping that her medical qualifications would allow her to live an independent life in America.

Writing these stories has been a process of sifting through letters and photographs, talking to family, making sense of what we remember and know, discovering what we don't.

Four of our mothers are still alive and have been involved in the writing, providing private photographs, letters and diaries, as well as giving lengthy interviews. Two of our mothers are dead and in the case of one, for over fifty years. She left behind just a handful of photographs.

We have written this book during the COVID-19 pandemic, sitting in different parts of the world – Japan, Costa Rica and Britain. Coming together on WhatsApp and Zoom, we have shared our professional experience as writers, editors, teachers and readers and created a supportive space within which to critique and develop our writing.

Through our individual and joint explorations, common themes have emerged, perhaps most profoundly the theme of migration – our mothers' migrations through countries and cultures, our personal migrations to deeper understandings of our mothers, our collective migration as writers towards a greater awareness of what binds us to each other and to our mothers.

We believe these stories are not ours or our mothers' alone. They are stories of all women in the world, stories of yearning for more, of courage to embrace but not to forget, of holding on, of letting go and of going back, of weathering the distance and of passing it all on.

MAKING A SHORT LIFE COUNT

Cathy Hull

Durham – London

My mother's life will never be recorded in history. Her life, like millions of other people, was only important to the handful who were close to her. Her story is simply told. She grew up in a colliery village in the North East of England to working-class parents. The Second World War gave her the opportunity to move eventually to London and she returned only briefly to her childhood home. Audie, as I knew her from my early childhood, wanted more from life than was available to her in her hometown. She wanted economic security and the opportunity to travel. She sought for herself an intellectual life amongst people who discussed ideas, and where she could explore her vibrant imagination. There can be no doubt this ambition passed from Audie to both of her daughters and subsequently to her grandson. This is all the more surprising as she suffered from serious illness all her life leading to her death at only 46. But her short life demonstrates that it is not the longevity but its intensity and richness which matters most. This piece tells the story of Audie's life and the qualities of her mothering that are of especial importance to me and that have, in turn, influenced my approach to mothering.

* * *

My mother, Audie, died just three weeks before my 18th birthday. It is now nearly fifty years since her death yet, as I write, my connection to her is as alive as ever. Of course, people we have loved live deeply within us long after they have gone as memories are triggered almost daily by what we read, hear or see. Old photographs, some with notes on the back, others eliciting quite specific recollections become especially evocative as time passes. But my mother's legacy is perhaps even more profound since, as my father Bill, who is still very much alive, often says: *"You are like her in so many ways"* – meaning in my character and personality rather than physically. So, although my biography is so different from hers I remain very much her daughter and, all these years on, she is my ever-present mother.

What I am seeking to do in this piece is to tease out and understand in what ways I am like Audie and what was special about our relationship. Of course, because of her early death, our relationship was almost entirely that of mother and child and never had the chance to mature as most mother-daughter relationships do.

In this piece, I am relying on memories which after so long are inevitably selective and are still being constantly reinterpreted because *"remembrance of things past is not necessarily the remembrance of things as they were"* (1).

The key point here being that we constantly create our identity through returning to our memories as we rewrite the stories we tell about ourselves again and again. The present is always suffused by the past and the past is constantly reviewed by the present.

This chapter is about the stories that I have constructed from my childhood and how my life has been shaped by them. I am including extracts from the many diaries I have kept which date back over a 40 year time period. These include notes of walks taken, of holidays, as well as letters and postcards received and sent. I have also drawn on the few family photographs I possess and which I have used to provoke thought and jog my memory, allowing me to dig down further into the past. I have been astounded by how much still lives deep within me. Experiences I had long forgotten have emerged like archaeological finds allowing vibrant, meaningful insights into what made my mother and what made me. These stories of my past have also provided different versions of what I thought to be true and new insights have emerged as the "dig" has progressed. Let me begin with a photograph:

In this picture Audie is sitting on a stone from which a rounded figure has been carved. She is looking sideways to camera with a smile on her face. The figure itself is enigmatic and I am not sure what it represents. It is holding its large belly and looks wrapt in thought. It's an easy holiday snapshot of a picture. I know immediately that my father is the person taking it because of the ease with which she is returning his gaze. She is smiling *with* him rather than at him and I can sense there is a shared joke between them. Audie is sitting, I feel deliberately, in a similar way to the statue suggesting a connection. What interpretation can I make of this photo? As I look more closely other thoughts come crowding into my head. I am taken beyond the photo itself and into a long-forgotten memory.

Audie is in her purple bobbly coat, the one with the big "drop-down" collar. It smells partly of the makeup she wore to cover up her complexion made blotchy by illness and as I draw closer into the memory I can smell Audie herself. To me, she always had a rich earthy smell similar to heather or thyme. I draw my breath for a moment to take it in and find myself moving deeper into the memory without being able to describe precisely what I see. I try and hold the moment before it goes and I return to the photograph. She is still there looking sideways to camera, at her Bill, smiling. They are both laughing at the figure, at its roundness, its sulkiness, its belly button. Audie is wearing her best shoes or what she called her "going out shoes". I know this because they have higher heels than those she normally wore because of what she referred to as her "bad feet" from the years of wearing ill-fitting shoes in her childhood. In this photograph, you can just make out her legs made bloated and puffy by illness. It is 1963, Audie is thirty-eight and we are living in Germany. The picture is taken at the Palace in Berlin. Audie doesn't know it yet but she has less than 10 years of life yet. You wouldn't know this from the photograph because today she is smiling at Bill and they are sharing a jokey exchange.

As I put the photograph down another memory comes into my mind. It is of Audie again in the same purple bobbly coat with its "drop-down" collar. Only this time I am in the picture. We are walking across a wide road and I am holding her hand and managing to skip at the same time. I am about five or six years old. I can tell this by my size and the pixie-like cut of my carrot top red hair, the coat I am wearing and my '*Lucky Two Shoes*' sandals. Today I am playing hopscotch and at each step, I jump in the air and shout out the name of a country within the United Kingdom. At the first jump I shout "England," at the second I shout "Ireland," at the third I shout "Scotland" and on the fourth, I leap even higher in the air shouting "Wales" as I land with a heavy thump on the ground. She is laughing with me and bending down to be close, buttons my coat and whispers something softly into my ear causing me to laugh out loud. It's a bellyache of laugh and she is laughing too. In that moment of bending down towards me the collar of her coat falls away from her shoulders and tickles my face, I can feel it now as I write this and it is in that tickling I smell Audie again. Her earthy, brown rich smell. It is a smell of time past.

But when it comes to our memories time is an illusion because *"inside the head everything happens at once. Reality resides in the mind" (2)* Memories are past and present – timeless if you like.

So, what is the memory here? What is the story being told in this picture? It depends, of course, on who is telling the story. If Audie could tell the story she would tell a different one. But for me, it is a simple childhood experience that can easily be understood. Its meaning lies in the moment when Audie bends towards me and I reach up to her. For this is the story of our reaching out to each other. I want to know what happens next. I want to know so much more about the woman in the purple bobbly coat with its "drop-down" collar sitting on the statue or bending down and inadvertently tickling my face. A collar that held a smell that I have inside my head to this day.

* * *

My mother was born in the small village of Sacriston in the County of Durham in 1925. In 2014 I returned there for the first time since I was a child. I was hoping to find something of the spirit of the village as it had been when Audie grew up there – or perhaps even something of Audie herself. But as my diary entry suggests the landscape of the village is now very different and there is little left of what animated the community in which my mother lived.

Diary Entry, May 2014, Sacriston, Durham

Today if you stand outside the house where Audie grew up all you can see are lines of early twentieth-century red-brick terraced houses and a view of rolling hills beyond. The air is clean and fresh, alive with the sound of birds. When I look out towards the field I wonder Is this the path she would have taken every day to school? What would she have seen? The field beyond my view is green, a deep verdant green that makes me want to run at it – rather than into it. Is this the field where one festival day Audie was kicked by a horse so badly she had to spend a whole year in bed? Is that old path the one she would have skipped along to the library?

I turn back to look at Audie's house and in that moment of turning I catch a memory. I have been here before. I know I have. I sense it deep within me. There is something for me in this landscape. I know this place. I am holding two visions in my head at once. The first is my outer vision – or what I can see directly in front of me on this day in May 2014. And what I see is the house with its reddened bricks, four windows and a door. In truth a child's drawing of a house with smoke billowing from its chimney. The second is my inner vision which comes from somewhere else. It lies just behind my eyes, a little more than memory but less than truth. I see Audie aged 18 or so, looking out from the top window of the house towards the town. She is also holding two visions in her head and what she sees is her present and future laid bare. In front is a sprawl of ugly colliery buildings, railway lines, trucks, and pit machinery blackened by the slag belched up to the pit head from deep below the ground. Was this to be her future?

Audie's father, Fred, was one of over 600 men who worked at the coal face whilst hundreds more worked above ground to move the coal to homes, factories and power stations across the country. The air was always black with coal dust with just the distinctive wheel on top of the pit head shaft standing out. Fred worked down the pit when the mines were in private ownership and health standards were poor. It was dangerous work and accidents were commonplace. Miners were exposed to poisoning from methane, carbon monoxide and dioxide as well as the long-term impact on their lungs from coal dust. Stunted growth, crippling injuries, skin diseases, arthritis, bronchitis and emphysema were all too prevalent. Attempts to improve working conditions – such as the General strike of 1926 when Audie would have been just over a year old, only led to defeat, lockouts and further reduction in wages and, during the depression of the 1930s prolonged periods of unemployment.

Mining families like Audie's tell the story of constant poverty and insecurity. Work could stop at any time because of poor health or mortal accidents. She grew up at a time of the most profound economic depression in the twentieth century. The hardest-hit areas in these depression years were the industrial and mining towns in the north of Britain. Fred, my mother recalled, would frequently "go on the tramp" (3) walking ten or fifteen miles a day looking for work during those years. Poverty "hovered as a belief" across my mother's childhood but she always stressed that she grew up in a happy family. Sociologists note that communities built around "extreme occupations" such as mining and deep-sea fishing where insecurity is a given, tend to be close and supportive with clearly defined roles in which the mother has pivotal responsibility. And this is true in Audie's family. Olive held it all together through thick and thin ensuring that Fred was always fed first before her or the children. Interestingly, throughout my childhood, even though my father always worked in white-collar jobs, Audie continued this family tradition and as children we were always made to accept that "your father comes first".

Religion also played a key part in coming to terms with the strictures of life in a pit village. It was something that brought the community together on both happy and sad occasions. Fred was a lay preacher and, together with Audie's mother, Olive, would be off to Chapel in the nearby village of Witton Gilbert every Sunday morning where he would deliver a sermon and Olive would belt out a hymn with the congregation. As has often been observed, there was always more 'Methodism than Marxism" in British working-class communities and that was certainly the case in Audie's village.

My father recalls that Olive was a talented watercolourist who generously gave him her own box of watercolour paints to encourage him to begin painting. He still treasures that paintbox to this day. None of the pictures survived but I understand they were delicate pieces depicting the local landscape and its flora and fauna. Wesleyan Methodists like Olive knew that education was a route out of poverty and she taught all of her children to read before they started school.

This photo was taken around 1956. I know that because if you look to the right of the picture you can just see me in my much loved Davy Crockett outfit with fur-tailed hat and tomahawk in hand. Olive is next to her youngest son, Clifford who is in uniform and she is cheerfully wearing his RAF hat in what looks like a "home on leave" photograph. Auntie Irene has her hand on Clifford's knee protectively and Basil the "middle" child is standing behind his mum. Audie is sitting slightly out of the picture with a radiant smile on her face. What a smile! This photograph shows that being poor did not lead to unhappiness or resentment, rather it strengthened close family bonds as they depended upon each other for so much. It was Olive and Fred's unselfish encouragement which supported Audie and subsequently Clifford to leave Sacriston and forge new lives for themselves – Audie to London and Clifford to South Africa, only returning for occasional family visits.

Diary Entry, 2014, Sacriston (continued)

I look at the house one last time craning to hear whispers from the past or at least sense a presence through the bricks. Many other families have lived here since then and all that is left today is silence. I return my gaze beyond the house – to those dappled green fields – the feet of my ancestors are there beckoning me to walk with them, to feel the swish and swirl of grass against my legs. I draw strength from the texture of this landscape – the pattern of its fields, the sound of feet on dirt tracked paths. Somewhere far below is the old moorland or farrowed lines of soil. Dig down a further 1700 ft. below and you will find men inhaling sulphurous air, their rasp and wheeze dimmed by the sound of iron flayed against rock. The fields stretch away, serene, but underneath lies the life of my ancestors. I dig down deep to find them. A homecoming of sorts then, – a sense of home.

* * *

Music was certainly a strong feature of Audie's early family life as it was when I was growing up. Both my parents were interested in music, especially my father who had a wide-ranging and oft-played record collection. Many are the times I arrived home from school to hear Audie and Bill singing away to songs being played on the radio. From the living room, Audie could be heard blasting out the words to the No.1 tune of the day, such as Guy Mitchell's "Singing the Blues" with Bill whistling the accompaniment in the kitchen. Audie borrowed heavily from the hymns she learnt as a child substituting the original words with her own. So, for example, the 1883 standard "*There Shall Be Showers of Blessing*" was rewritten to include the verse: "*There shall be showers of blessing, showers of blessing we need, Kate's socks around us are falling, for some suspenders we plead,*" at which point Audie would collapse on the floor in a fit of uncontrollable laughter. The lay preacher's daughter was anything but pious or sanctimonious.

When she was aged around eleven Audie was badly wounded by a horse. All her life she had a large hollow at the top of her leg. This resulted in her spending a whole year in bed with nothing else to do but read books. This turned out to be her "year of magical thinking" (4) allowing her to discover different worlds, learn about places and people leading lives very different from her own. Reading gave her new perspectives on the world. One of the less celebrated social reforms of the mid-19th century was the Public Libraries Act of 1850 which by the time Audie was growing up meant that most families lived within easy access to the local "lending library". Audie and her family made good use of this and I can imagine her immersed in her library books curled up in bed in her red brick home in Sacriston.

By the time Audie finished her schooling the economy was recovering not least because of the stimulus of the War which opened up opportunities for that whole generation of women. In particular clever women like Audie were encouraged to consider secretarial work which was seen as considerably superior – a "cut above" – domestic or factory work. Audie had grown up at a time when women were often expected to work until they were married, but then return to the home when they had children. However, the War changed everything and the expansion in clerical work provided new opportunities for women. In order to escape from Sacriston, Audie needed to become economically independent and self-reliant. Although plagued by ill health an excellent command of English enabled her to secure coveted work in the Civil Service and she was soon posted to Worcestershire, a distance of some 230 miles from Sacriston as part of the War effort.

In truth, I know very little about Audie's life during the War. She was 18 when she arrived in Worcestershire to start her clerical training with the Civil Service. I do know that it is around this time that she made a decision to lose her Durham accent. It is hard to imagine how significant this was back in mid-twentieth-century Britain when strong regional accents – particularly northern accents – were anything but de rigueur as they have become today. Whilst the term *accent* refers to how we pronounce words, the term *dialect refers to* the different varieties of the same language that have evolved in different cultural or geographical locations. The dialect spoken in Sacriston is very different from that used in Southern England. Everyday "Geordie" as it is called was partly developed out of working life in the colliery reflecting the landscape and cultural life of the region. An example of the strength of the Geordie dialect is clear in the sentence: "*The gadgie's tannin proper radgie*" which simply means "That man's extremely cross".

In choosing to speak differently, then, Audie had to find new words and phrases from the very different environment in which she was now living. Most people who learn a second language retain at least some of the colloquial words and phrases from their first, but Audie did not. The only way people discovered she was from the North East is because she told them. She was not ashamed of her northern, working-class background, nor did she try to emulate the cold, clipped tones of the English upper and middle classes of the time, which to modern ears now sound so false. Rather, she developed a beautiful speaking voice and used her newly acquired accent to express herself well and in her own unique way. I can still hear her voice on an old reel-to-reel tape recording that my father made in which the family created our own radio programmes for what we called *Radio Berry* – Berry being my family name. It was just a bit of fun, but it magically captured my mother's speaking voice and the natural and quite unaffected classless accent she had adopted. But I still loved it when, for my entertainment, she would revert to her broad Durham accent.

Towards the end of the War, Audie was posted to Kensington, London, where the Civil Service had requisitioned Barkers department store. She was housed in one of the many "women's hostels" which had been set up to accommodate civil and military personnel posted to London during the War. And so it was at a dance in Kensington Town Hall in 1948 Audie met my father, Bill, and in October of that year, they married. In this photograph of their wedding, Audie is wearing the up-to-the-minute, post-War *"New Look"* style for women and Bill is in a smart double-breasted suit, his shoes carefully polished. They lean into each other and even from this faraway lens I can sense their happiness, share it even, because I know these people. I have lived with them all my life. She is 23 and he is 22, the War is behind them and a new life stretches out ahead. There are several others in the picture some of whom I recognise. To the far right is my father's sister, my Auntie Shirley, and next to her is Grandma Clara – my father's adored stepmother. But there are others I do not recognise at all. How important are they to Audie and Bill's story? They do not appear in any of our future family albums. They belong in the past, to Audie and Bill's life before I was born or even imagined. But in this moment of happiness, they are part of my parents' story. My parents do not know their future, they might imagine it or even plan it yet they cannot know it. But I do. What I do know of their life before this picture was taken and before I was born I have tried to weave from the facts and stories that I have heard and been told and beyond that from what Audie has passed on to me as through a kind of metaphysical umbilical cord. So that if she were to read this piece she would come to recognise herself in it. Just as a mother knows her child – can smell her, sense her, feel her even when she is grown, so too the child knows her mother – but only if she cares to look. The two young people in this photograph – Audie and Bill are in part responsible for who I am because their influence upon me has been profound. They do not know what the future holds for them. But I do. I long to freeze this frame beyond the photograph, to hold on to that perfect moment of happiness for them.

* * *

They both said it was love at first sight. It is easy to see how different Bill was from the men Audie would have met in Sacriston at that time. Born in London my father has always been more "city" than "country". Within weeks of meeting each other, he was introducing her to London. They bought a tandem two-seater bicycle and regularly cycled across the City to take in the sights, my father complaining that *"she was always on the back with her feet up so that I had to do all the hard pedalling. Cheeky monkey."* He said, "We just clicked." They shared the same passion for literature, music and art. My father has often remarked that *"Your mother was clever. She was different to most of the women I met. She was interested in anything from history to philosophy and we both shared this love of reading.*" But for all her intellectual interests she was never stuffy. Bill said, "*You could always make her laugh – we could make each other laugh,*" and apart from a brief period in which they lived with Fred and Olive to save money, Audie never returned home.

Audie had malfunctioning kidneys and suffered from renal failure all her life. After my older sister was born, doctors advised her against having any more children. Yet despite this, she was elated when she found out that she was pregnant with me, later recalling that on hearing the news she boarded a red double-decker London bus, climbed to the top deck and rode around and around the City in a quiet reverie of excitement. As I grew up I came to appreciate that my mother's choice to have me – despite all warnings to the contrary – made for something special in our relationship. We developed a unique bond based on our shared passions and ways of seeing the world. We spent enormous amounts of time together on our own, especially in the last two years of her life when my father was away working and my sister had left home to start her nursing career. The closeness and intensity of the mother/daughter relationship which developed between us I can now see as having the most profound impact on my life in the many years since and on my own mothering. Motherhood is so much more than juggling the day-to-day practicalities – demanding as they are. In a much deeper sense, it moulds and shapes children's lives – hopefully for the better. Certainly, in my case it was very positive in countless ways. Perhaps this is best illustrated by some of the most vivid memories I have from those early years.

So, for example, I can vividly recall how I would rush out of school as soon as the bell rang, my shoes squeaking as they hit the pavement, spurring me on. I wanted to be home in double quick time, so would run as fast as I could until I was panting so fast I just couldn't breathe. Once through the door, I would throw my satchel on the floor and head for the kitchen, leaping clumsily onto the kitchen table, my back against the wall and legs straight out in front of me:

"Go. Go. GoGoGoGoGo!" I would shout. "Go!"

Audie, expecting me, would be all calm and without looking up from stirring the pan she was minding would continue her story from where she had left off. So in her best storytelling voice, she would begin:

The two sisters are in bed. Little sister opens the drawer in the bedside table and takes out a necklace. It's made of squares of glass threaded together so that when she holds it up to the light each piece seems to hang in the air as if floating – as stars in the sky. Except this is a necklace of mirrors. Their colours constantly change under the refractive light. Ruby comes first, followed by cranberry then crimson. Blues and greens turn to turquoise and then to dandelion yellow all sparkling in the skylight. These glass pieces tumble out of the sky and hang just above their bed.

"Your turn," said big sister. "You go first"

And without a pause, the youngest reached out her arms as high as she could, up and up she reached – higher and higher she went until she could feel her fingertips touch the shards of glass from which she could draw the necklace slowly towards her until what had been a mere colour began to take shape. Soon her attention came to focus on just a few colours, perhaps four or five at most.

It was the browns she was drawn to, with their rich caramel smell of sugar cane and earth making her want to dive right inside the glass. And that is exactly what she did. "Corr!" She said when she opened her eyes because she found she had not dived INTO the earth but was walking on top of it, along the side of a small field of green shoots. She was barefoot and her feet squelched on the wet earth below. "Corr!" She said again, delightedly, pushing her feet further and further down into the soil as hard as she could to feel more of the rich squelchiness. "This feels like the squelchiest squelchy I have ever squelched in."

It is that word "Corr!" that does it. Corr? Corr? That long-forgotten English word from my childhood. "Corr!," a word through which others come tumbling into my head in every shape and size, words from my childhood that quickly become stories – Audie's stories about Jersey cows that wore striped jumpers, of upside-down trees that were too lazy to bear fruit, of naughty children who never did what they were told and, for me, most memorable of all, a glass necklace that you could climb inside if you closed your eyes and pulled the thread tight enough.

Audie's stories awakened all my senses, making me aware of colours, tastes, smells, sounds and the very feel of things. Today a country walk can excite Proustian memories of childhood – the smell of Autumn leaves, the excited chatter of sparrows, the rustle of trees, the gentle patter of rain on the leaves of a beloved oak or ash tree, or the feel of moss beneath my toes. Audie taught me to look, listen, hear and feel the world. I guess today some might see this as a kind of mindfulness but for me it is an ever-present awareness that makes life so rich. It is this that I would pass on to my son, Tom.

Audie drew inspiration from her stories and colourful vocabulary, her her wide reading, which ranged from Chaucer to Shakespeare to dazzling stories from *The Tales of the Arabian Nights*, or classic nineteenth-century literature such as *Wuthering Heights* or American crime fiction writers such as Raymond Chandler, Dashiell Hammett and Ellery Queen. These texts are not uncommon and many people read them today. But for Audie, they fired her imagination and introduced her to new words and images, and the wholly different world of "broads" and "juke joints" and where everything cost a nickel or a dime. Audie and I would read these stories together often moving outside of the text as we adopted the appropriate accent, or rewrote our own sentences from that written on the page. She always wanted to bring the stories to life so that sometimes she would move swiftly through dense text to something which she knew would delight me, or sometimes embellish it to make it heighten the intensity. Indeed, she had no fear of changing the words in the sentence of a book to make it *read* better without simplifying its language or the meaning. This of course increased my interest and since that time I have returned again and again to the books we read together, reading them more slowly to find new things to be discovered within them.

Audie loved words and in a very modern sense exploited their boundless possibilities to be rewritten, re-invented and re-imagined. Today her own stories might seem simple and naive but as children we lapped them up. Words for Audie were about so much more than just meaning but also about their capacity to evoke smells, colours, tastes or indeed anything which excited the senses. Is it any surprise then that I love reading fiction and particularly the kind that can conjure up vivid images, sensations or feelings? My mother's broad tastes in her reading have also encouraged me to reject the crude distinction between high and low culture, or what Angela Carter has described as legitimate and illegitimate literature. Audie loved Dashiell Hammett and Shakespeare or Dickens equally. Fiction was, for her, simply a "place to dance and sing"(4). Those days sitting on the kitchen table enthralled by Audie's tales shaped me and my passions in a way she could never know.

But to see Audie as just a dreamer or creator of fantasies would do her a great wrong. Rather, her story is one of courage. Her move from the poor and restrictive environment of a pit village echoes that of any migrant today. Southern Britain was more affluent and had suffered much less than the north of England during the worst of the depression years. Then, as now, London and the "Home counties" surrounding the Capital were almost a distinct economy and society which sustained a much richer and more cosmopolitan way of life. Community was not a given as in the village in which Audie grew up. Rather, city life was made up of a host of overlapping communities to which you had to become accepted. Some who moved south never made the transition and returned to the north as soon as economic circumstances allowed – to be back in more settled communities which they found "friendlier". Indeed, to this day people who grew up in the north often comment on the unfriendliness of "Southerners". However, Audie enthusiastically responded to the challenge of making a new life. Although shy she soon made friends and put people at their ease as she fashioned her identity.

That said, our home life still retained so much that was typical of post-war working-class families. We lived on a diet of stews designed to eke out the meat through the week for as long as possible. Jam roly-polies, custard and other sugary food made up our "afters". Like all women of her generation, Audie was a good seamstress and she sewed many of our clothes, although just as often we lived in "hand me downs" or jackets that were too big for us with the hope that one day we would grow into them. Sometimes a parcel would arrive from Auntie Shirley in America or Audie's youngest brother Uncle Cliffie now living in South Africa. America, particularly, was more affluent than England in the post-war years, so it was always exciting to open Auntie Shirley's parcel full of clothes for my sister and me and usually a lipstick for Audie. After opening our parcel my sister and I would "dress up" in our "Auntie Shirley dresses" and together with Audie, Bill would take us out for a day in our newly acquired Ford Anglia.

She passed on to me the then working-class values of stoicism such as "standing on your own feet" because "nobody will do it for you". She never used her illness as an excuse to avoid a challenge or shirk responsibility. My mother's work ethic has stayed with me my whole life. These were qualities that certainly sustained her and our family as we moved from place to place.

My father's work for the Ministry of Defence (MOD) meant that we moved every three years and were expected to live with RAF personnel on a military base. We lived in officer accommodation. In those days the divide between "officers" and "other ranks" was marked and carried within it subtle and sometimes not so subtle distinctions of class and status. What was important was rank. This must have tested Audie's adaptability as she was now mixing in a very different world from the one in which she had grown up. I have a photograph of her at a rather formal Christmas dinner in the officer's mess. She looks beautiful in her brocade cocktail dress and delicate brooch pinned at the font. Bill casually turns to camera, his arm leaning informally across the back of Audie's chair. But in reality, these events would definitely not have been her thing. As always, her good humour and simple grace would have carried her through. She never warmed to the rather cold and over-polite way of military life amongst the officer classes. Audie observed people and together with a high emotional intelligence she understood people and the subtleties of social interaction. This would have helped her to empathize with people. In her own quiet way, she was popular: as Bill once said, "Everyone loved Audie. They just *loved* her."

Our peripatetic lifestyle continued throughout my childhood and adolescence as we moved from one place to another including postings to Germany and Northern Ireland. Germany, interestingly was what had excited Audie's imagination as a child and my father said he took this posting especially to please her. She was around 11 when she wrote this in her diary:

'*Koln Cathedral is tall with two spires. It looks to me like a fairy tale castle. I wonder who lives there. I would like to visit Germany when I grow up. It has a Black Forest! It has lakes. I would like to visit when it is snowing*'

Although this is a simple sentence, it shows that at a young age she was already imagining a world beyond Sacriston.

* * *

We were living in Northern Ireland when my mother's health seriously deteriorated and she wanted to return to England so my father accepted a job in Cardington, which is a small village to the south of the town of Bedford. Bill had no choice but to begin work immediately and before our new house had been made ready. So for much of the final year of Audie's life, she and I found ourselves alone together. By this time she was increasingly immobile and so we would spend our time talking and sharing stories and books together and so we grew close. I believe it was one of the happiest periods of both our lives. We arrived in Cardington just as Audie's illness took a turn for the worse and we had begun to spend more time reading together. One day, she suggested that we read Wilkie Collins' long novel *The Moonstone*. I am not sure what fascinated her about this particular book and I was doubtful about reading what she herself referred to as a doorstep. With her declining health, I was aware we might be forced to abandon it mid-clue without discovering the outcome. But its importance was simply in the two of us reading it together and sensing my hesitancy Audie said softly:

"You worry too much. We can reach the end if you just read faster!"

This of course was a reminder of how little time we had left together, and keen not to disappoint I felt a sudden urgency to begin. *"Can I,"* I asked myself, *"squeeze more words into each minute? Yes! Audie is right, I just need to read faster!"*

For Audie reading was not something to be done passively but an active stimulation of all her senses, intellect and imagination. It required mental agility and as she grew increasingly tired we decided to take regular breaks between reading to allow her time to rest and for me to catch my breath.

There could be no doubt that she was hovering in that liminal space between both being *in* and *outside* of the world. Now, all that was available to her beyond the daily grind of pain was her memory of a life once lived and an undiminished ability to imagine the world. So, in the very process of dying what became ever more apparent was her unquenchable passion for life.

Her bedroom had never been a place of illness but a social sphere where family came together at its most intimate and honest. It was as untidy as life itself. And so, that first afternoon I opened the door to a bed strewn with flimsy typing paper covered in blotchy, faded violet letters and a chewed pencil with its worn-out rubber tip on the table nearby. At the foot of the bed was a typewriter, cast aside for now and balancing precariously near the edge. I imagine it now as a 1930s Remington Bluebird with a chrome manual return lever and italic letters embossed on top of each key. In truth, it was probably the more recent Imperial Good Companion, a pale green portable just light enough for her to haul about the bed. Its fat, plastic button keys would have felt slower than the Remington Bluebird which must have been a great irritation to her as at best she could reach a top speed of around 55 words per minute. It was from her rapidly moving fingers that ideas dropped 'clickety-clack' onto the page, arranging them-selves into carefully constructed quirk stories.

This particular afternoon she was propped up on pillows as I settled myself next to her before opening the first page of Wilkie Collins' gripping tale:

One of the wildest stories related to the yellow diamond. A famous diamond in the annals of India..."

"A yellow diamond?" said Audie. *"Wait. Read that again."*

This was typical of our usual pattern of reading as we shared our thoughts and sometimes made wild digressions before returning to the text. In her last days, we were still on a journey together. Now, so many years later, I understand that this was her final gift to me. We never did get to the end of the story. In many senses you never can. Yes, you can read them to the end but when you return to them years later they so often appear to have new meanings and quite different outcomes. Perhaps one day I will finish The Moonstone.

A few short weeks later Audie died. My father moved for another posting and my sister had already left home to take up her career. I was 17 years old and on my own.

* * *

Now, fifty years since Audie died, I am trying to understand the influence she has had on me as a person in my life since, and upon my mothering. I am exploring this by revisiting the many diaries I have kept over the years which detail both the ephemeral and more significant elements of my life. The diaries go back as far as 1977 and have continued to the present day. These entries were not written to be read by anyone other than my immediate family and therefore are often constructed without concern for grammar but written in their original form in a rush of excitement to capture a particular moment, experience or emotion. The fullest diaries are those I made on our holidays when as a little family of three we spent golden days enjoying time together. They catalogue a host of inconsequential memories but taken together reveal so much about what mattered to us as a family and as I can see now – reflect the abiding influence of Audie. Not just my son Tom, but also my husband Vernon got caught up in the way we created stories out of our holiday experiences. So, for example, rescuing baby turtles struggling to get access across a beach to reach the sea became a story about how years later one of those little turtles – now a very large turtle – rose up from beneath the waves to rescue Tom whose boat was sinking. And there were many more. These stories always had a child-like simplicity to them which of themselves were fun to create. But they were more than just a fun family activity because they harboured within them two vital principles which guided Audie's stories as well as our own. One is a belief in the power of telling stories. The other is the recognition that fiction in the broadest sense is simply a vehicle for shining a light on different aspects of people, the world and beyond. Through reading fiction, we can move beyond our own worldview and gain new insights and perspectives. Whenever I have found myself alone I turn to fiction because it is populated with interesting and entertaining characters who absorb my attention and in a very real sense remind me that I am not alone.

Audie wrote stories because like most writers she was interested in people and liked to look, listen and observe them. I am the same, and my diaries are filled with observations from listening to snatches of conversations, noticing how people interact, sit, or look and inhabit their environment. All of this was handed down to me from Audie and I believe it is this that has been passed through me to my son, Tom. To illustrate this, here are two very different extracts from my diaries written sixteen years apart. The first is taken from the diary I wrote when I discovered I was pregnant with Tom and shows how for me observing the natural world so often correlated to my inner self. The second was written 16 years later and I hope captures the way in which we subtly observe each other whilst capturing the essence of an inconsequential afternoon interaction.

Diary Entry, New Year's Day, Bedford 1982

It's New Year's Day and we are in Bedford visiting Vern's relatives over the festive break. This morning we are taking a walk along the river which stretches the length of the town. Our starting point is from the elegant 18th century Swan Hotel which overlooks the river. We have decided to take the "road less travelled" and heading in the opposite direction to the Victorian embankment to the east we cross the main road before slipping down the side of an old bridge to the water's edge. To keep us warm from the hoary snow we begin our walk with a brisk spring in our step. An ice-cold wind slashes hard against our faces awakening mine to make me rally against its sting. I look at V, whose face is deep ruddy red with cold. He claps his mittened hands together and walks on invigorated.

It's a painterly day. Everything is in paintbox colours – the cobalt sky deep blue tinged with silver that catches the tone of a winter sun, drawing low across the river to splash light across the water.

I catch sight of a bank of reeds across the bay cut through by the harrowing wind, they stand stark and alone. We stare out caught by their blackness. Their stillness. A stillness so profound I move slightly to check its truth. And in that second I feel a movement within me. Stroking me. And I slide my hand inside my coat and stroke my belly and acknowledge another truth.

Our feet crunch on the muffling of snow on bracken or twigs. The smell is of that rich moist-wet-clean-wet-dirt-brown smell that makes you want to stand still. Drink it in. I draw breath again and again breathing the raw earthiness inside of me.

In spring and summer, the path is overshadowed by trees through which the high sun is filtered making lacy patterns to decorate our route. Today the trees are leafless, their skeletal branches bared hard against the cold. There is something magnificent about winter trees. Sculptural. Without leaves they form windbreaks to cheat the wind of its whorl and whoosh. They calm the day and keep us warm. We stand for the longest time looking up, tracing their shape as far as we can. Higher and higher we look until reaching up with our fingers to seize the day.

"I used to come here as a kid," V says excitedly. "See? Just over there," he said pulling me close so I can follow his pointing, "look just beyond the old boathouse. Yes, there. We'd fish for, well, sprats really," and in his moment of pointing his voice trails away as he turns in upon a memory from his child-hood. Memories are like fishes that can suddenly tug the line.

I leave him there and charge swiftly on, snatching the moment leaving the riverbank to plunge into myself. Walking does that to me. It takes me both into the world and out of it providing the creative dialectic and rhythm that I need.

Today I am thinking of Audie. It is ten years to the day she died and where, less than a mile from here, we scattered her ashes, her "clinker" as they call it in Durham I walk faster at first and then, as if propelled by thought itself, I begin to run, faster and faster I go, like a sprinter with arms moving in time with my feet and heart pulsing. I hear V shout: "Be careful!" But on I go with this child dancing inside me. And then suddenly I stop. The memory evaporates, it is impatient to be gone, for now at least. She has passed the baton on, I think. It's my turn now. She will be back. She will want to see my mothering.

We continue our walk, V's arm protectively through mine. Across the river, a few swans shelter by the bank. They too are waiting for spring. A comely sight lowering their necks down beneath the water, searching for food. I push my hands down further in my pockets and we move forward slowly. A happy family day. Audie just behind.

In 1998 Tom is sixteen and my diary tells of a day I spent with him in Canterbury:

Diary Entry, Canterbury, 16th June 1998

I am 44 going on 64! I am looking at my jean-ed self in the mirror. I wish I was one of those women who know how to dress, who can throw a scarf over their shoulder and look fabulous. I have never been like that. I enter the kitchen sighing as I walk.

"What's up, Mum?" Tom asks

"Oh, yer know. Look at me," I say doubtfully, disparagingly.

And so we found ourselves driving to Canterbury on a dull Saturday morning in June. Canterbury is a Cathedral city with a maze of higgledy-piggledy streets and more than a hint of history. On the right day it can be beautiful, and a walk around the City walls can lead you quickly back into the past. But today it is dull. Now it's a "destination tourist" city which at a weekend can be writhing with people filling its cafe bars and restaurants. But we are not deterred. Tom makes straight for a shop that takes his fancy "here Mum, now!" He exclaims enthusiastically as I flick through racks of clothes "try THESE on" – a simple pair of grey tartan trousers and a red jumper. Except they are not simple. The cut of the grey with its light embossed colour, the material and shape of the jumper are natty little numbers and very far from what I would usually buy.

"What…Me?" Oh well, what does it matter? So I try them on and we emerge half an hour later with two cardboard clothes bags. Half an hour is all it took to change me.

We are both happy. I with my new purchase, and he with his new ability to dress me! And so it was on a dull day in June with the crush of tourists upon us we found ourselves inside a nondescript cafe, just one of the main chain of cafes that populate this town.

We lean back in our chairs both aware of it, that small hint of something different, a move beyond, a hint of change. For his choosing wasn't childlike, rather it came from an adult with a sense of knowing, of being able to look objectively at me, assess and see. He knows this is a moment. He doesn't know what it is or what it means. But I do. He slides further down into his chair 'til he's way down low and slowly takes a cigarette from a packet and lights it. He doesn't look at me – except he does. What will I do? I do nothing. I do not tell him to put that cigarette out at once. It will kill him or at the very least fill his lungs with puff and clag. "Put that cigarette out now." No, no, no. I do not say that. I hold on to the moment. I stare down at my coffee and then look up and say "Do you know the poem 'All Things Must Pass' by Lao-Tzu?"

"No?" I try and say it, badly as it happens as I have forgotten all the wonderful dots and dashes, twists and turns of the poem. Not 'til later did I

find it. For now, though, we sit together sharing our silence. No longer mum and son. But you and I, I think.

Driving home later in the rain. I say **"You mustn't smoke. It will kill you and at the very least fill up your lungs with puff and clag."**

Now I can say it. The moment gone. He knows this, understands it and smiles.

"No worries, Mum, I don't smoke that much anyway."

A week has passed and there is a book on my bed **A POEM FOR THE DAY**. *In it is the poem by Lao-Tzu and on the inside of the front cover is this:*

'To Mum,

Keep this with you all the time.
Read each poem line by line.
Think of us in Canterbury High Street.
Matching eyes and matching feet.
Your red jumper, me looking smart.
In new grey trousers, looking a tart.
Beautiful rain highlights your face.
Red Rouge Cafe. We stare into space.
We can make pictures from every day.
Having adventures, being stupid anyway.
When we're together it will never end.
I'm not with my mum – that's my best friend.'

In this extract from my diary, I detect a direct line from my mother, through me and on to my son. Two mothers and three lives connected by a common understanding, a shared belief in words, communication and stories.

* * *

In many ways it is Audie's early death that has had the most lasting impact on my life because it shattered family life as I had known it. My father, Bill, had a nervous breakdown within weeks of her death and when he eventually recovered moved away and I lost contact with him for many years. My sister became a naval nurse and my contact with her was also very limited. What became clear is that Audie had been at the heart of our home and when she died our family died too. So just a few months after

Audie's death I found myself living on my own, in a town I hardly knew and with only a few newly found friends. It is only when looking back at this time that I have come to realise how isolated I was. At an age when most adolescents are beginning to take the first steps to becoming more independent, I had independence thrust on me. I was close in age to when Audie had also left her childhood behind and yet began to create a new life for herself. But she had a family. I had none. In this time of crisis, I turned again to Audie for support. She was the person I carried within me, guiding and reassuring me as I created a new life and identity for myself. Being Audie's daughter I stood on my own feet because as she herself had told me " *No one else is going to do it for you.*" Mirroring Audie within a few short years I had settled down, completed an undergraduate degree and, just ten years after Audie's death gave birth to my son, Tom. Of course, I have had many more opportunities than were available to women like Audie at that time. There is no doubt, for example, that if she had not been born into poverty she might well have gone to university. But her life, as with many other women of her generation, showed me how to become a strong, independent woman. She was there when I walked onto campus on the first day of study, six years older than the average entrant. But whilst most "freshers" were worried about missing family and making new friends, I strode across confident and excited with a photograph of Audie and my husband Vernon folded carefully inside my bag. And from that moment I never looked back – just like Audie when she boarded the train from Sacriston to London.

Like my mother, my own life has had something of that of a migrant. Most migrants will tell you that when leaving home their journey was focused on the future and the hope of a better life. But in making that journey they have lost part of themselves as they leave their past behind and *"efforts to reclaim that which has been lost result in something more than nostalgia, but if you are lucky less than exile. For migrants, losses keep coming. Funerals, graduations, christenings, weddings missed and where there are no family members present to validate your experience."* (7) And there's the rub. For can I place Audie in the photo of my graduation? My subsequent academic successes? The birth of her first grandson? My wedding? Migrancy can, of course, be a positive experience especially if you are well received when you arrive. And in this sense I was lucky too because I did not leave. I was still living in the country of my birth and recognised as such. I soon created my own home and family. But what was lost was my sense of knowing or being known – of belonging to a family, since my own family had quite suddenly disappeared.

Writing this chapter has been as much a process of discovering where I am from, and my identity, as it is about my mother. In exploring Audie's life I have had very little to go on, and am only too aware of the faultiness of memory, the extent to which we all remember or at times misremember our past. The danger in relying too much on memory is how quickly it turns into nostalgia and, for me at least, a yearning to return to an idealised childhood. In writing about my mother I have had very little to draw upon apart from a handful of apocryphal family stories and photographs. Initially, I began by attaching to these imagined truths and giving them deeper significance than they deserved. But I have come to question this and to realise that they are simply memories of family life. Family tales are those told and re-told by different members of the same family until an accepted version is agreed by all, and repeated regularly at family gatherings until it passes into history as truth. Although they are the warp and weave of family history other stories often lurk behind them if you care to look because how can individual family members arrive at the same truth? And to ask questions in this way also means you have to question the story you are telling and in so doing revise it. The story I started out to tell here has changed in the writing and is not used just to make sense of the past but to create a different version of it. As we grow older we return to memories and recreate them again and again; after all, "the past is a foreign country, they do things differently there" (8).

* * *

In 2019, when she had been dead nearly fifty years, I decided to have an apple tree planted for Audie in the cemetery where her ashes had been scattered so many years ago. The diary entry below records my first visit to the tree.

Diary Entry, August 2019
To reach Bedford Cemetery you first have to walk through the Park. When it was constructed in the late nineteenth century over 18,000 trees were planted so that on our walk through it today they form a shady arch through which we progress towards the Cemetery. This adds to our contemplative mood and we slow our walk to enjoy this arboretum all the more. A visitor would wonder at our constant stopping to smell the pine or, more than often to look for the longest time at the aged Oak.

Bedford Cemetery was opened in 1855 and is set in around 37 acres of land. It is no longer open and perhaps because of this still retains some of its Victorian charm. Here and there are dotted a few beautiful Victorian Angels, their wings pointing upwards, perhaps to guide the deceased to heaven. But today I have no time to look at these wholly because I am focused on finding Audie's tree. The cemetery office is closed so we do not have a map to find the orchard. We are forced to pick our way around the graves towards where we think it is most likely to be found. We linger over several gravestones wondering who was "John Hill" and whose hearts was he "always in"? Or of Maud Graham, 1821-1899, who died over a hundred years ago and yet her grave today has been well-tended. She continues to be loved. By whom I wonder. What place can someone so long dead hold? Who is the witness of Maud's life or death here? What are the stories beneath these headstones? These ruined piles of rubble. The people here had mothers that loved them and many had daughters too. Daughters who sat down at these stones and wept for time missed, for memories still held, and to ask "Why couldn't we have had another a week, another month – another fifty years together?" Why so soon? But ultimately, this is not the point, surely? What matters is the time we have lived – what we did and what we gave in life. And, of course, what we leave. I see V signalling that he has found the orchard and I am in a hurry to be gone, tripping over the many headstones felled into the earth. I am walking over dead bones to get to you, Audie.

The orchard is small and newly planted. Perhaps 20 trees in all. In truth these tiny saplings are merely leafless scraps of twig. Curiously, this makes me smile because it means Audie's tree will continue to grow – will be here at least as long as I am and perhaps long after I have gone. She will outlive me. What joy!

The Cemetery Trust have stipulated we are only allowed a small plaque with the name and date of birth of the deceased written on it. And so in our search for Audie's tree we stop at every one and read each name out slowly. I feel a rising panic as we come to the last two trees.

"She's not here," I say to V, "they have it wrong."

"She will be here." He smiles.

My panic is not that she won't be here. The panic is that she will – how will I react? After all "It's been 50 years. It's gone. I won't cry a bit. It will be joyous" I say and in saying this catch V's wry smile. He knows me well. And then we find it. The label on the tree says it is a variety called 'SUNSET'. "SUNSET!" I say. "How funny! Are you laughing, Audie? Of course you are!" "SUNSET?" I hear her say.

And then a simple black plaque: "Audrey Ivison Berry 1925-1972." She is here after all. The tears come immediately, falling down my cheeks, through my hair, down my neck. They gush from me as a river. I am watering her tree. *"This is not her grave,"* I say at last because we have brought her into life. This tree is a life-giver. Soon apples will grow on it to be eaten up and each year new fruit will follow. I feel a quiet keening within me – a lament for all that is lost. I look at Vern.

"I knew you would," he says, laughing at my tears, drying them with his hankie. And I laugh too my mood lifted. We move away from Audie but before I do I take a final look. I will return. Next time the tree will have grown and borne fruit.

* * *

1. Proust M, (ed 2003) *In Search of Lost Time*, Penguin Modern Classics

2. Lively, P, (1987) *Moon Tiger*, Penguin Modern Classics

3. Steedman, C (1986) *Landscape for a Good Woman*, Virago Press

4. Didion, J (2004) *The Year of Magical Thinking*, Harper Perennial

5. Carter, A (1992) *Wise Children*, Vintage Classics, New Edition

6. Frost, R, *The Road less Travelled*.

7. Younge, G (24th March 2015) article in the *Guardian* newspaper: "As Migrants we leave home in search of a future, but we lost the past."

8. Hartley, L P (1954) *The Go Between*, Penguin Classics

LOSING MY MOTHER TONGUE

Rupal Shah

India and England

My mother has given me many gifts over the years, some of which I loved, some I rejected, some irritated me and some I didn't notice. But all of these gifts have mattered, especially the ones I didn't ask for and which I wanted to give away. Her way of expressing her love is not the same as mine; she shows her love through doing, I show my love for my daughters through words. But that isn't important. The love I can give my girls comes from having known all my life that I am unconditionally loved, even when my mother and I have been unable to reach each other and it feels as though there is more that separates us than binds us. I was born in England, grew up speaking English, reading English books and then married an Englishman whom I met when we were barely adults. So my 'Indianness' isn't the same as my mother's, but it is still a part of me and so is she.

Soil and Soul by Rowan Rheingans, Songs of Separation

> 'To soil and soul.
> Soul and sea.
> What will we leave when we leave?
> What will we lose, if we lose?'

Sunshine streams through the inner courtyard of the family home. A girl about 7 years old, thin and serious, wearing a clean cotton dress with two neatly oiled plaits reaching all the way down her back sits cross-legged on the floor with her older brother, helping him with his homework. He has missed a lot of school because he is a sickly child and his father will be angry with him if he doesn't catch up soon. Her younger brother and sister are playing in the street outside, from where noises tumble into the house, of laughter and chatter, dogs barking, the ringing of cycle bells and the chanting of prayer. There is a scream as a street cow headbutts a child who has wandered in front of her. However enticing these sounds, the girl knows that she is needed inside – that her own mother still only 25 years old bears the burden of being a wife and of running a household consisting of four young children and a husband who is exacting and unbending. So when she finishes studying with her brother, she will help her mother with the cooking and then as dusk gathers, she will light oil lamps so that the family can see as they eat their evening meal.

At least that's how I imagine my mother when I sit on the same floor many decades later, in the same house, in a different world.

My mother, Sarla Vaidya was born in 1941, in a medium-sized town in Gujarat, the state to the north of Mumbai. This was in the middle of the

Second World War, which was straining the already weakened relationship between Britain and India to breaking point. The union was finally severed just six years later, when India finally declared her hard-won independence. When my mother was a small child, there were several British government officials still living in the vicinity. It was a different, sepia era. She was the older girl in a family of four siblings, one younger sister and two brothers.

The house where we still stay when we visit India is a typical Gujarati house, made up of 3 storeys arranged in two interlinked columns centred around a large open courtyard, a room at the front and back of each floor with dark, narrow staircases and a roof terrace. Electricity came to my mother's town when she was eight but was erratic while she was growing up – oil lamps were still widely used. Running water was available for only an hour each morning and the children had to help their mother to fill buckets to last for the rest of the day. There were virtually no cars and most people either walked or cycled through the narrow, cow-filled streets. Each street or 'Pole' was a community in its own right, with strong, long-established connections between the families living there.

My grandfather, 'Dadaji', was a doctor who practised both Western medicine and Ayurvedic medicine, a popular combination with his patients who wouldn't have accepted a purely Western approach. Ayurveda is an ancient Hindu practice that relies on combining treatments based on herbs, minerals and metals with certain dietary and lifestyle rules and is still practised in India today. There was never any doubt as to who was the head of the family. My grandmother, 'Ba' never challenged his authority. He was seven years older than her and far more educated; she had grown up in a small village, whilst he had gone to university in Bombay. It was a traditional, arranged marriage and Ba was considered very fortunate to have such a husband. Her duty was to serve him. My mother observed their marriage every day. She adored her father but little trickles of doubt still flowed into her mind when she saw how little agency her mother had. Perhaps this subconsciously influenced the decisions she made later on for her own life.

Dadaji was highly disciplined and unbending and he expected to be obeyed by his wife and children. Even into his late eighties, he went for a 10-kilometre walk every day and ate only one meal consisting of dhal, vegetables and a handful of rice. He was stick-thin until the end. Dadaji was renowned throughout the town where they lived and by association, his family were held in high regard. When they went out, my mother remembers that they would always be greeted by grateful patients; and she and her siblings were treated with respect, bordering on reverence. She developed a deep awe of her father the healer, which she never lost while he was still alive and which often left my own father feeling wrong-footed and inadequate in her eyes. Dadaji was an ever-present but invisible presence in my childhood, setting the bar high, unyielding, implacable, always right.

Dadaji was a fervent supporter of his venerable Gujarati compatriot Mahatma Gandhi. Gandhi advocated a pared-down, ascetic lifestyle. So Dadaji's children were taught to value duty over individualism, studies over play and to mend or make rather than to buy. As a young man still at university, Dadaji participated in the 1930 Salt March, an act of civil disobedience in which thousands of Indians led by Gandhi marched to the sea to make their own salt, as a protest against British taxes and the British monopoly on salt. The march started off with only 79 of Gandhi's closest supporters, but attracted hundreds and thousands of people from different castes over its 240-mile course, culminating eventually with the arrest of Gandhi.

Unlike today, it was an era when simplicity and home industry were close to the Nation's heart, a way of rejecting the shackles of colonialism and of reclaiming its identity. The idea of 'dharma', which loosely translated means the right or dutiful way to behave was a prominent influence in India at the time. My mother's disposition was suited to this outlook on life and she became her father's favourite, dutifully devoting herself to school work, helping my grandmother to manage the household and caring for her older brother who was frequently unwell with chest and ear infections when they were young, before the time antibiotics became freely available in provincial India. There was very little importance assigned to what any of the children might want individually, much more to their place in the family and community. The importance given to duty, predicated on the existence of clear rights and wrongs, strongly shaped my mother's outlook for the rest of her life. It was a way of thinking which suited her, or perhaps it didn't occur to her to question it. This wasn't the case for all her siblings – her youngest brother was frequently chastised by Dadaji for staying out too late, lost in a game with his friends instead of spending extra time on the schoolwork he hated.

Life followed a familiar pattern with few surprises and few outside influences. The family didn't own a television until well after my mother had left home. She did well at school, but to her bitter regret not well enough to gain a coveted place to study medicine at a local university. My grandfather was not willing to let her travel to study in a different state, worried she wouldn't be safe as a woman living by herself away from home – there was no way to argue against this decision, so she resigned herself to reading chemistry at Bachelors and then at Masters level in the local college. This is where she met my father, who was one of her classmates. He was of a different caste to her, something which would usually be quite a barrier to a relationship, were it not for my grandfather's belief in Gandhi's ideology – including a rejection of the caste system, which divided people into social groups based on their historic professions. My mother is a Brahmin, a member of the caste of priests and teachers, while my father is from the lower Vaishya caste of merchants.

My mother as a university student

In spite of the difference in their social backgrounds, my father was struck by my mother's looks and self-containment, she seemed to him an elusive and unattainable figure. He began to pursue her, waiting to cycle back home with her after college, much to her dismay. She had lived a sheltered, puritanical life so far, in which even the idea of romantic love had not figured at all. She was confused and annoyed by this new turn of events, especially by the teasing from her friends which resulted from my father's courtship of her. She wanted to be left in peace to continue her studies and made this clear to him, despite his persistence.

In the end, discouraged, my father accepted a scholarship to study for a PhD in the UK and left India for London in 1965, thinking that he would be back in a few years (this expectation lasted well into my childhood before it gradually faded from conversation). He didn't forget my mother though and continued to write to her and ask her to marry him. Finally, both she and my grandfather began to come round to the idea. It was a small town and everyone knew about their involvement, making it hard for my mother to move on, even if she had wanted to. Even the faintest scent of scandal lingered in those days, driving away potential new suitors.

By this time, she had finished her Master's and was teaching chemistry to undergraduate students in Ahmedabad, the Capital of Gujarat.

'There was a gentle, regular rhythm to the days. Mum, you have told me how you would wake early, bathe and eat with Ba and Dadaji and your younger brother Ashok, who was still a bachelor living at home. Whatever you ate would last you the whole day. What was the point of spending money on food if you didn't need to? Much better to stick to nice, clean home-cooked meals. Dadaji would walk you to the station. You describe how the streets were still subdued but seemed poised to unleash their tumult as the new day took hold. Your journey involved taking the train and then the bus. You always chose the carriage reserved for ladies, wanting to avoid unwelcome stares and the men who would 'accidentally' bump into you. Once you were chased by a rogue cow, all the way from the bus stop to the college. You had to run, your sandals slipping off, tripping over your sari, much to the amusement of your colleagues and the students. But that one angry cow was the source of the only hostility you faced when you were working there.'

My mother was in her late twenties now and her prospects of getting married were diminishing rapidly. At the time, most girls would marry in their early 20's and she was viewed as an old maid – her own mother had married at 17. Remaining a spinster was not a particularly attractive life choice, involving caring for elderly parents while never having a family or home of her own. She capitulated to what seemed in any case more and more inevitable, fated almost. My father's family helped with the marriage negotiations and ultimately it was settled that she would fly to London and marry dad as soon as possible after that. It was highly irregular that she should first join my father and marry afterwards –if he didn't honour his promise, she risked ruin. She had never even been outside Gujarat let alone India and the whole prospect felt extraordinary to her. However, ties with England were much closer then, with Indians allowed to settle here as Commonwealth citizens. Moving abroad was a prize which many people aspired to and this made my mother feel more confident about her decision.

Sarla Vaidya, soon to be Sarla Shah, sits in the 'ordo' with her mother Lila-vati. The ordo is the room at the very back of the house, used to store rice, lentils, flour. There is no natural light and the only furniture is a wooden swing which they both sit on now. The smells of the stored food intermingle with the spicy aroma of the meal they have just eaten together. It is evening, the household chores are finally complete and the heat of the day has abated somewhat. The weak electric bulb on the ceiling does little to attenuate the darkness of the room.

Sarla will leave for London in a week. The die is cast, there is no turning back. She looks at her mother who is not yet 50 but whose face is lined and who already walks with a stoop which will become more pronounced over the next decades of her life. Lilavati never had the opportunity to study – all her choices have been made by men. It has been a hard life but these are her golden days, her reward for all her earlier efforts. She has daughters and daughters-in-law to help share the work, her husband has grown to love and respect her over the years they have spent together, everybody in the neigh-bourhood likes this sweet-natured woman who has followed her dharma as a dutiful daughter, wife, mother and now grandmother.

Lilavati is crying at the thought of losing her daughter. To comfort her, Sarla shifts position so she is lying like a little girl, with her head in her mother's lap, wiping away her own tears. She thinks of all the sacrifices her mother has made which she hasn't had to, of how her life is so different already from her mother's; and how it will diverge still further when she leaves. She doesn't realise yet how much.

Flights at the time were ruinously expensive and my father hadn't been able to afford to come back since he first left, so she hadn't seen him for 5 years –not even a photograph. She didn't know if he would be the same or if his time in the West would have changed him. She was only too aware though that once she got to London, it would be too costly to return in the near future. She was signing up to a change of life without a clear idea of what this meant.

There are very few photos of either of my parents as children, but there is one of my mother and her younger sister, taken when they were about 12 and 10 years old in a photography studio in Ahmedabad, the state Capital of Gujarat. Who could have predicted that the little girl with the earnest expression, who so clearly belongs to India would be the first of her family to emigrate; would end up travelling halfway around the world, never to return permanently and would bring up her own daughter in a foreign country, speaking a foreign language?

My mother aged 11 or 12 with her younger sister

In the end, after the long process of getting a passport and arranging practicalities, she arrived at Heathrow in October 1970, when she was 29, with equal measures of trepidation and hope for her future in Britain. It was considered a desirable place to live, the common belief being that moving here would bring material success and the associated trappings of wealth. As a Commonwealth National, she was entitled to come, told she would be welcome; and she trusted this message. But she didn't know that Britain had a deeply ambivalent relationship with her new brown and black citizens. No dogs, Blacks or Irish. The signs weren't on display anymore since the Race Relations Act had been passed a couple of years earlier but the feeling was still there, simmering just below the surface, painful sparks erupting unexpectedly.

My mother knew intellectually that Britain's climate would be very different from India's, but she had never experienced a day without sunshine until she arrived here. When I think of India, I imagine bright colours, the smell of incense, the clamour of people and of course, the heat. In Gujarat, it is very unusual to have a day without some sun, even during the monsoon season. Mum had never before experienced the sensation of feeling cold – even in mid-winter, the average temperature is 20 degrees Celsius in her hometown. It was physically shocking to step into the damp, greyness of an October day in London with only an inadequately thin cardigan which she wore over her sari, looking for the man she would marry, taking in her adopted new country.

By the time you arrived, dad had been in London for 5 years. This is how long you had been apart and you say that you weren't sure what to expect when you landed at Heathrow. Five years is a long time to keep the idea of someone in your mind and heart. You felt that the image of my father had become blurry and indistinct. But your heart lifted with relief when you saw him waiting for you at the arrivals gate, even if his rounded stomach was new and unexpected. When he held your hand, you were shocked to take in the smell of smoke. When tears came to your eyes, you didn't know if they were the result of happiness or sorrow.

Mum and dad hadn't exchanged photographs during their separation. She felt completely at a loss as to how to greet this man she used to know and whom she would now have to marry. Not doing so would mean returning to India with a reputation in tatters, the shame of living with this in a small community and almost certainly no remaining marriage prospects.

My father had become accustomed to the British way of life and was enjoying the freedom of living alone without supervision. He had grown up with more independence than my mother, being the oldest boy in his family and having a stepmother who had her hands full trying to look after her own children. He had the big advantage of having a near-native grasp of English – his father had been an English teacher and he had grown up with English being spoken at home. He had read many English novels; PG Wodehouse was his favourite author and formed his first notions of Britain. His experience of London was therefore very different from my mother's. He remembers it in the main as a friendly, welcoming place and recalls how often he was engaged by strangers in conversations about Nehru – Jawaharlal Nehru – the aristocratic, Cambridge-educated first prime minister of India, who understood the British upper classes so well, who was imprisoned by them but who was the lover of Edwina, the wife of Queen Victoria's great-grandson Lord Mountbatten.

The images of London in 1970 which emerge from the stories of my mother and father are so different that it makes it hard to believe they are talking about the same place.

So at the airport, they were almost strangers again. He had moved on, she hadn't, but they were irrevocably bound to one another.

My parents' wedding day

Those early days in London were hard for my mother. Although she had studied English at school, she found she could understand virtually nothing that anyone around her in East London said. The vernacular of Walthamstow had little in common with the old-fashioned, formal English she had been taught. So it wasn't that she had no knowledge of English, it was just that what she knew was of little practical use to her.

When she and my father had their registry office wedding a week after she arrived, she didn't know what the Registrar was asking her so she just nodded at what she hoped was the right time during the marriage ceremony. She supposed that when the registrar finished speaking, she was married, but wasn't absolutely sure. Weddings in India are typically multi-day events, with hundreds of guests, attending amidst an explosion of colour and noise. Even now but especially then, they are symbolic of the union of two families rather than that of a man and woman alone.

The contrast with her own wedding couldn't have been starker. My mother had none of her family at the ceremony; she had no relatives of her own in the UK and knew nobody. She was wearing a plain white sari, which my father had advised her to bring with her from India, instead of the vermilion which more usually adorns Indian brides. White is a colour associated in India with funerals, not weddings. They couldn't afford to go on honeymoon, an idea which didn't exist at the time in India in any case, so they simply went back home afterwards. A wedding in India belongs to the whole community more than to the individual couple, so it wasn't surprising then that my mother didn't feel as though she was really married.

The difficulty she faced with the English language was probably my mother's biggest struggle when she moved here. It was before the expulsion of Indians from Uganda and there were relatively few Indian migrants in the UK. This thin young woman wearing a sari, with a single plait that reached down to her thighs was viewed as an oddity, in a way that my father never was. Her lack of English was often interpreted as a lack of intelligence and she was patronised and looked down on, or at least that was how she felt. Given the elevated social position she had enjoyed in India, this downward catapulting of status was a bitter pill to swallow and had a permanent effect on her outlook and feeling towards England and towards herself. If identity arises from the relationships we have with others, my mother's sense of herself was under fire and I am not sure that she ever recovered fully. She felt that she wasn't seen as she really was and this, in turn, affected her ability to see the good in her British neighbours. A bitter pill to swallow, with a sour aftertaste.

Her first home in London was a shared house in Walthamstow in East London. Mum and Dad lived with another Indian family, but there was little common ground, as there was no shared language. My mother hated the indignity of not having her own kitchen and of having to share a bath-room with strangers. She had grown up with the Hindu notion that bodily fluids are associated with pollution, taking one further away from a state of spiritual enlightenment. It is hard to describe how demeaning it would have seemed to her to be forced into the intimacy of shared living with people she didn't know.

It was extremely difficult to find the ingredients she needed to prepare Gujarati food. This posed a real problem for her, on two counts. Firstly, unlike in other regions of India, the diet in Gujarat is strictly vegetarian with even eggs being taboo. Unfortunately for her, vegetarianism was very unusual in England in 1970, although it was gaining ground amongst the 'hippy' community which was of course very influenced by India.

But whereas hippies might have been humoured and tolerated, for Mum, being vegetarian was just another marker of being different. There was a butcher's shop in the vicinity of their house and she was filled with nausea every time she walked past it. Its very existence confirmed to her the essential barbarism and otherness of the British. Secondly, food plays an integral role in Ayurvedic medicine, which my grandfather practised –maintaining the correct diet is considered to be a vital part of the treatment of disease. This inextricable link between food and health is fundamental to my mother's beliefs and its significance for her is something I have struggled to understand. Food has always caused arguments between us – even as a child I remember feeling confused by the force of emotion which was unleashed if I refused to eat what she had prepared for me.

A balanced Gujarati diet is comprised of vegetables, rice, dhal and wheat-based chapattis or puris. All six flavours (sweet, sour, salty, pungent, bitter, and astringent) should feature during the course of a day. There are also various dietary rules. For example, fresh produce is considered essential. Cold food and drink are thought to be unhealthy. Particular foods should not be ingested simultaneously, for instance, bananas and milk. Historically, Gujarati women spent a significant percentage of their day in the preparation of food; and at the time, 'outside food' from restaurants was viewed with suspicion, particularly amongst Brahmin families (much like outside influence generally). My father had long since relaxed his approach to food. He had tried to stay vegetarian when he first arrived in London but had found it impossible, so had lapsed into eating meat some time ago. It took years before my mother would allow him to bring meat into their kitchen. My mother has always had the belief, passed down to her from her parents, that making food at home from scratch is essential for health and for her, it is an expression of love. Even now, she doesn't really approve of eating in restaurants.

Living in the shared house was obviously not working. Every night, there were arguments and tears. My mother was completely isolated during the day when Dad was at work and miserable by the time he got home. Within a couple of months, Dad had relocated them to a different house, owned by a Gujarati family, who were happy to sublet a bedroom to them. Mr. and Mrs. Patel were kind to my parents. Living there was much less lonely for my mother, who now had someone to talk to when Dad was at work. She stopped crying so much and put on some of the weight she had lost in those first few traumatic weeks. Mrs. Patel knew where to get the ingredients needed to make traditional Gujarati food and their house felt at least somewhat like home. Mum started to attend English classes soon after this, but found them to be too basic for her and was insulted by the assumption that she didn't know even simple grammar and vocabulary. This theme of feeling misunderstood and undervalued has been recurrent under various guises during her life here. She stopped going to the classes after a few weeks and I remember her still talking with fury about them many years later, when I was a small child.

Despite the language barriers, Mum was starting to get used to public transport – it would be several years before they could afford a car, a moment of triumph and celebration when it finally happened. My father's sister, her husband and baby daughter were their only relatives in the UK and often at weekends they would make the long, complicated journey by bus from Walthamstow to Edmonton.

Mum was delighted when she got her first job about 6 months after arriving in London, working as a laboratory technician in Baird and Tatlock, a firm making chemicals and scientific instruments, conveniently based in Walthamstow. She found the work easy, though expressing herself was harder. However, it was life-changing in terms of giving her a purpose and some independence. She experienced both kindness and cruelty – people mocking her accent, but a sympathetic boss who told her he was impressed by her work. Her eroded self-confidence healed a little. At work, she had to get used to greeting her colleagues by shaking hands or with a verbal acknowledgement. She was accustomed to the traditional Indian salutation 'Namaste', spoken with hands brought together, palms facing and bowing slightly at the waist. Namaste literally means 'the divine in me acknowledges the divine in you', and is intended to signify two souls meeting one another, a feeling which had been missing since she left India.

Sarla Shah nee Vaidya sits shivering slightly on the lower deck of the bus that takes her to work, pulling her cardigan more closely around her. She sits pressed up against the side of the bus, so that her sari doesn't overflow onto the next seat. The bus is filling up as it heads down the High Street so that the only seat left is the one next to her. Two English women get on and glance around. They see her sitting there and pointedly remain standing, although she shimmies across, to take up even less space. The first time this happened, she thought little of it, but she realises now that it isn't because people here prefer standing to sitting. She thinks she should be pleased to have more room to herself and tries not to mind. But the voice inside her head tells her "These people hate you and look down on you. How did you, the doctor's daughter come to be sitting alone on a draughty, rattling bus on the other side of the world?"

Men with long hair, women wearing mini-skirts and smoking, flares, alcohol, drugs. These are just some examples of the differences my mother encountered – Gujarat is a dry state where alcohol is illegal. She says she was often unsure of the gender of people she passed on the street. This was of course before the internet brought familiarity to people separated by geography. London was foreign to her on a level she couldn't have imagined. My father firmly felt that they had to assimilate if they were to make any kind of life in England. He encouraged her to cut her hair and to swap her sari for jeans. After his years in England, he felt more comfortable with this version of her. In fact, she probably wouldn't have got the job at Baird and Tatlock if she had arrived at the interview dressed in a sari. Even today, that would be a bold statement; in the 1970s, it felt impossible.

Starting her first job in London was an important part of my mother's assimilation into her new life in the UK. She slowly came to understand the unfamiliar, to carve out a place for herself here. It was significantly easier in the 1970s to get help with housing and to be offered assistance with rent. A social worker supported their application for a housing corporation flat, which they moved into in 1972. Having her own space again and no longer needing to share a kitchen was life-changing for my mother. She spent long hours cooking again, in the same way she had done back home. Having their own place also meant that it was possible to start thinking about having children and putting down more permanent roots. I was born while they were still living in this flat, before they nervously took the plunge and bought their own small house.

Assimilation can mean different things to different people. When it is gradual, perhaps it reflects the slow change in identity which is a natural part of the immigrant experience; a merging of the old influences with the new. When it is forced and abrupt, it can feel discombobulating and traumatic. Did my mother adopting Western clothes and customs mean that she was now English? How much do these external trappings matter compared to what is felt inside? In many ways, it was in my mother's best interests to make some changes to her appearance and behaviour, in order for her to be able to survive in London without being completely dependent on my father. But the very fact that she needed to do so made a difference to how able she was to assume her new identity.

In an effort to continue the process of assimilation, I was brought up speaking English as my first language, though I could always understand what my parents said to each other and to me in Gujarati. When I was growing up in the 1970s and 1980s, being Indian was something to keep hidden and I felt no incentive to embrace my Indian heritage – in fact, I was keen to stamp out any differences between myself and my friends at school, so that I would be part of the group. I was always aware that this required extra effort on my part, but I accepted it as part of life without questioning it, as children do. Perhaps acceptance in childhood is always contingent, requiring an understanding of the implicit rules of the playground. I felt that for me, it was especially precarious, liable to being withdrawn if differences which I tried to keep suppressed accidentally surfaced. I didn't understand then that ignoring my Indianness would leave a gap that it wouldn't be possible to fill later.

So by the time Margaret Thatcher came to power in 1979, ushering in a brave new world of individualism, my mother had moved halfway across the world and spent a decade living there, had gone from wearing a sari to jeans, from speaking Gujarati to English and from being single to being the mother of a child who didn't share the same first language or culture as her. Although I have visited many more countries than she has, none of my journeys compare to what she did.

My mother had a difficult delivery with me and was in pain for some time afterwards. She lost weight again and cried a lot in those first few months. I am sure that today, she would be diagnosed with postnatal depression. I was born in October and I don't know how she filled the dark winter days that followed, in the small, oppressive flat with no family except my dad, acquaintances rather than friends, no car and very little money. Bleak, cold days. No way to change the course of her life. No words to articulate the loneliness. She has always hated the cold, something we have in common.

My dad, not knowing what else to do, agreed that she should return to India with me for some months. He worked overtime so that they could scrape together the money for the airfare. There are a few photos from that time, with me as a chubby baby smiling in the sunshine, being held by grandparents, aunts and uncles. Mum is in some of these, wearing the po-faced expression favoured in those days when being photographed. Mum and I stayed in India for six months, soaking up sunshine and her family before reluctantly returning 'home'. I wonder if she was tempted to stay.

My mother didn't work again until I was old enough to go to school. In India, if a mother is unable to look after her baby, she calls on family members to take over. A baby is in any case part of the whole family rather than just belonging to its parents. As this wasn't an option, Mum felt that she needed to stay with me.

Me with my grandparents, Ba and Dadaji

The smell of dhal percolates through the house. We are in a two-up, two-down terrace on a quiet street in a suburb of North East London. Some of my earliest memories, hazy around the corners and unreliable. A 1970's fawn and orange patterned carpet, a Formica sideboard, a brown sofa I liked to jump up and down on. Juxtaposed with pictures of Krishna on the walls and rangoli in the entrance hall (coloured powder sprinkled into patterns to signify welcome). Suitcases balancing on the tops of the wardrobes in Mum and Dad's bedroom, packed with saris and shirts, as if we might decide any minute to beat a hasty retreat back to India. These are the things I think I remember. Watching cartoons on television followed by dinner, a bath, prayers and stories from the Mahabharata or Ramayana before bed.

Every Hindu family will have a small alcove in which they place images or statuettes of the Gods who are especially important to them, with accoutrements such as incense sticks, a small bell to accompany the chanting of the prayers, offerings of sweets and vermilion powder to anoint the images of the Gods after the prayers are finished. The words of the prayers, the ringing of the bell and the smell of the incense were at one time part of me. Now that it has been almost 30 years since I left home, they have become detached, part of a different life, slipping away unnoticed over time. I can't remember many of the words of the prayers, but the rhythms are still familiar and on the rare occasions when I hear them now, something long-buried resurfaces and is then lost again. Like the smell of incense. I never intended to leave these rituals behind, it just turned out that way. I wonder whether these almost forgotten times are still part of me or if it really is as though they never happened. They are a link back to somewhere I only remember as one remembers the taste of a meal eaten a long time ago, whose flavour lingers.

'My mother cooking in the kitchen, her hair tied back severely in a pony-tail. I can tell from the tone of the plates and cooking utensils being banged together whether she and Dad have been fighting or not. Along with the smell of spices, it seems to me that there is the taste of emotion in the kitchen. It fills me with a vague sadness I don't understand. I tend to avoid the kitchen and read a book in my bedroom instead, a pattern which continues throughout my childhood and teenage years. There are questions I want to ask, a gulf I want to cross, but I don't and I can't. There are some things that can only be said in your mother tongue. Besides which, I fundamentally dislike the high level of expressed emotion in our house, especially when it spills out in the presence of my friends, causing me acute embarrassment. It is messy and loud, it doesn't make things better as far as I can tell. I want to avoid releasing anymore, so I withdraw, dissociating myself from it and observing. I used to think of this as arising from a natural reserve, but now I think that really it was born from a child's instinct for self-preservation. I want to retreat to somewhere private. Feelings are not something I want to discuss, I know even then that they pass. I would rather remain concealed and blend in -anonymity and acceptance are what I crave. I wonder whether my mother tried to reach me despite this and how it felt for her when she couldn't. A hard, insidious process of moving away, too elusive to pin down and name.'

The medical room at my primary school smelled of disinfectant, I remember white walls and a grey laminate floor. The nurse was a large woman with flabby jowls and curly brown hair. She wore a plain white uniform as if to camouflage into her surroundings.

'Mrs. Shah, I am afraid your daughter has head lice.' She frowned, glared at us and raised her eyes to the ceiling before speaking very slowly and deliberately.

'You must use this special shampoo for three nights in a row. Do you understand? It's very important so that the other children don't catch it.

Please don't bring your daughter back until you are sure they are gone.' I imagine a slight smirk on her face.

My mother swelled with rage, scrabbling for words to help her to express her rage.

'There is nothing wrong with my daughter. You are an ignorant woman. Even if the lice are there, I will make sure they are gone by tomorrow.'

'Well, what extraordinary behaviour, I have never been spoken to in such a way. Absolutely extraordinary.' The nurse was red-faced now and looked as though she had been slapped. I wanted to die and wondered if there was any way to make myself invisible. My mother pulled me out of the nurse's room and marched away still fuming to herself.

At the time, I was convinced that mum had over-reacted hugely and inexplicably. Now I see it wasn't about the lice.

After the years of veiled insults, you became adept at recognising people's true meaning even when it was cloaked in half-smiles and polite expressions. You could always tell when someone didn't like you because of the colour of your skin, but you couldn't express yourself and so you got angry. I hated that growing up, I used to wish that you would just let things go and not draw attention to yourself. You were braver than me and didn't mind voicing your outrage, whereas I buried mine deep inside.

My first day of primary school is indelibly etched into my memory. I was younger than the other children, because my parents had somehow persuaded the headmistress that I should be allowed to start early since I could already read. As a solitary only child growing up in the suburbs, books were a treasure trove to me, opening up new, exotic worlds and giving me new perspectives on mine. I really loved our local library, the musty smell that hit me when I walked in, the quietness, the vast choice of books (or so it seemed to me), including old favourites that evoked particular feelings or memories. Both my parents made every effort to take me there and never hurried me away. The adults I came across looked at me approvingly, which didn't happen that often in other contexts. When I was four years old, I couldn't imagine a better job than being a librarian. Education for Brahmin families is of the utmost importance and my mother took mine very seriously. She strongly encouraged my love of reading, even though for her it served a different purpose, more about betterment than pleasure.

Some of my favourite memories of childhood are the frequent trips with my father to a large Central London bookshop, where I was allowed to choose any books I wanted. When I chose badly, he withheld judgement. This liberality of spending didn't extend into any other aspect of life; our food was simple and inexpensive, our rare holidays were spent in cheap hotels somewhere in the UK. It gave me a sense that books were essential to life. Ironically, giving me such unfettered access to worlds where English children picnicked and had adventures took me further away from my mother in some ways. I wasn't able to share with her the joy that I found in the stories. But I think she knew. She always read to me at bedtime, until I didn't want her to anymore.

My mother and father were both determined to learn to navigate the British education system so that I wouldn't miss out on any opportunities. There was no question, ever, that I wouldn't take these opportunities and make the most of them. That was why they had moved to London and it was why they stayed. She and my father had absolutely no doubt that I could and would shine academically, one of the few things about which they were in perfect agreement. This was not constraining to me, I was happy to accept it. In fact, it produced a certain confidence which was missing from many other aspects of my life; one of the only parts of my identity which was certain and didn't generate confusion and mixed feelings.

School felt so foreign to me at first, although it was only a hundred metres from where we lived. My life before this had been more Indian than English. What I remember most is the food. I had no idea what it was that was being put onto my plate that first day of primary school and I would have cried except that I didn't want to attract the attention of the teachers. There was a grotesque purple pudding that made a lasting impression on me. Looking back, I think it was probably rhubarb crumble, my husband's favourite food, something he associates with his childhood. I moved it around my plate and hoped that no one would force it on me. I had never eaten anything except Gujarati food before. In the end, Mum made me daily packed lunches so that I could avoid these strange new culinary experiences, which she was as suspicious of as me. There was a tea party once, at the house of a school friend. I was repelled by the fizzy black drink which was meant to be a treat. In the dying days of the 1970s, a working-class child from Ilford didn't score any points by admitting that she was only used to drinking water.

When I started school, Mum found a job as a laboratory technician in a secondary school, assisting chemistry teachers to set up equipment for the practical lessons in the chemistry lab. I went to a childminder after school. Bunsen burners, safety goggles, gloves, aprons, hard wooden benches, chemicals. That particular smell of science reminds me of her and of myself as a small child, when I went with her to work. I spent days during the summer holidays playing in the school labs, which seemed highly exotic to me, hiding under the benches, wandering through the classrooms, imagining myself a teenager, starting as a pupil at the same school.

With her Master's degree in chemistry, my mother always felt that it should be her giving the lessons, not simply helping to set them up and ordering equipment. Eventually, when I was eight or nine years old, she embarked on a post-graduate teaching course which she did one evening a week at a university in Central London. So on Thursday evenings, I had to stay late at the child minder's house after school, waiting for Dad to collect me. We would walk home via the sweet shop and he would buy me a necklace of sweets and a magazine, then we would curl up and watch television, eating food my mother had pre-prepared. I was allowed to stay up until she got back home because it felt so difficult to fall asleep without her in the house. She really struggled with the essay writing but she stuck at it and doggedly rewrote assignments that were returned. Sometimes she would ask me whether a particular sentence or phrase made sense, I was her interpreter because I understood what was expected and what would sound right.

She did get through the teaching diploma in the end though and eventually found a teaching job, albeit with some difficulty. After a series of rejections, she was told by an interview panel: "We know you have the right qualifications, but to be honest, we are concerned that you haven't ever taught in a British school before."

Frustrated and exasperated, she retorted, "Well someone has to give me a chance, don't they?" She got the job and taught chemistry in that school for almost 20 years before she retired. I think that was her proudest achievement and she never lost sight of the difficulty she had faced getting there. She always approached her job with great enthusiasm and never minded marking homework in the evenings or planning lessons at the weekends. Brahmins are traditionally supposed to be priests or teachers, so maybe she felt that she fulfilled her destiny in some way.

While my mother was embarking on her new career as a teacher, I began secondary school. As had been the case at primary school, there were very few other Indian students and we viewed one another warily, understanding that forging friendships with each other might threaten our acceptance into the wider group. My path had been set. I didn't enjoy school, but I didn't find it difficult. I watched with detachment as other girls went out with unsuitable boys, took drugs, got drunk or pregnant. However much our paths were diverging, I knew that to rebel would be to capsize the fragile boat my parents and I sailed in, leaving them to drown. It wasn't a possibility, so I didn't entertain it as a realistic option. I left home at 18 to go to medical school, a decision that delighted my mother whose dream it had been to study medicine. I never lived at home with my parents again. At university, I found common ground with people from many diverse backgrounds, including the boy from Yorkshire whom I later married.

My mother has always seemed to me to belong to a different generation, a different time – whatever stage of life we are at.

And now she really is an old lady, almost 80 years old. It strikes me powerfully, like a blow when she stumbles as she walks or when she mislays words or faces. She doesn't dye her hair as often, so now it is a random collage of white, black and grey, with the white winning out. They moved away from the terraced house where I grew up to be nearer us, swapping their house for a flat. In the end, she lived in that house longer than she is likely to live anywhere else. Dad's plan to move back to India one day never happened. When he boarded the plane to London in 1965, it turned out to be a one-way ticket.

They both adore their granddaughters. My mother's relationship with her grandchildren is lighter than her relationship with me. There is less baggage and fewer shadows, leaving lots of room for love. She has helped to look after them from the time they were babies and they are very close to her. The girls are firmly rooted in their British identities, there is no question of where they belong. Their father is English, able to trace his family back for several generations to a particular part of Yorkshire. It wouldn't occur to either of them to question their right to be here. And after all these years, Britishness has crept stealthily into my mother's soul, so that she too has become more British than Indian. Now, when my parents go to India on holiday, they look like foreigners. My mother hasn't worn a sari or shalwar kameez for years and instead wears a short-sleeved shirt and trousers. Her hair is cut into a long bob. Mum and dad are both taxed by the heat, by the noise, by the lack of a comfortable bed. They grumble about these discomforts and imagine themselves back in the cool comfort of their home in London. When they go shopping, they are offered tourist rates much to the indignation of my mother. "But I'm an Indian. I'm from here," she says crossly in English to the sceptical shopkeepers.

Mum and Dad have mostly stayed indoors since the coronavirus pandemic struck. He still goes for a walk every day but she hasn't left the flat for several weeks.

'When we call, her face is frightened. She listens to the news several times a day, though we tell her not to, is aware of the increasing death rates from the virus. She wonders what will happen to her and to my dad, how and when it will all end. I encourage her to leave the flat to go for a walk but feel apprehension at the thought that perhaps this advice is ill-judged. But I can see that she might become entirely housebound by the end of this if she doesn't go out. On their roof terrace we face each other, separated by a distance of 2 metres.'

It is 1982. We are on holiday in India, for the first time since the months spent there when I was a baby. Mum planned for this trip assiduously, diligently buying presents for everyone in the extended family. It was a time when many consumer items were not yet available in India, so bottles of talcum powder, perfume, lipstick, chocolates, aftershave – even socks – were highly desirable commodities. There was an implicit expectation that anyone returning to India from 'foreign' would distribute this largesse to all their acquaintances. Finally, the ever-prepared suitcases were coming into their own.

I remember my parents quarrelling about how much this was all costing. And at the airport, anxiously waiting to see whether they would be pulled up on their generous interpretation of the luggage limits. I hadn't wanted to go with them. When I visualised India, I imagined poverty, dirt and disease; those were the images I had seen portrayed on television. I didn't feel any curiosity about this country to which I apparently had invisible ties. As far as I was concerned, it meant that I had to have several painful immunisations, was forced to take bitter tablets which I struggled to swallow to protect me against malaria and missed several weeks of school.

We landed in Bombay, as it was still called then. We needed to take an overnight train journey to Nadiad. Bombay Central Station seemed to be a microcosm of India. The maelstrom of noise, the smell of food being sold by vendors and general chaos overwhelmed me, so I was surprised that my parents seemed not to notice how alien it was. We arrived in my parents' hometown very early the next morning. I was mainly focussing on not vomiting as I got off the train, so I was taken by surprise when we were met by many people I didn't recognise but who turned out to be my family. Dadaji and Ba were part of the entourage.

Everyone seemed delighted to see us, even me whom they didn't know. My grandmother covered me in kisses, tears streaming down her face. I struggled to know how to respond, I only just recognised her from photos we had at home. I had a sense that I might cry in reciprocation but I didn't. There were familiar names being called, people I had grown up hearing about without ever having met, suddenly embodied. It was like being in a vivid, slow-motion dream. My mother was swept up into a sea of faces, hugging some, touching the feet of older relatives to show respect and having her own feet touched by my cousins and her younger brother and his wife. I noticed the respect with which everybody addressed my mother. She was an educated woman who had made a life for herself in a new country and they were proud of her.

It was so hot, even that early in the morning. India rises early, so the roads were already filling. There was the excitement of getting into a rickshaw, bundled high with people and luggage, precariously speeding through the crowded alleyways, a miracle that nobody got hurt.

My first glimpse of the house where my mother grew up. Meeting my cousins and feeling like a giant compared to them. An oafish, inept giant who dressed differently and who could only speak to them clumsily, with the vocabulary of a toddler. Nonetheless, they were all so kind and called me their sister. I had never been a sister before, though I had always longed to be. Children see their parents in relation to themselves. I had judged my mother for not fitting in, for being different and in my solipsistic way, for the consequences this had for me. When I looked at her then, enveloped by her family, I saw that she wasn't how I had imagined her to be. She was sitting cross-legged on the floor, fondly ruffling the hair of her older brother, now a middle-aged, bespectacled man, who had once been the sickly boy she had cared for when they were children. I understood briefly that my version of her was only part of the truth. I had an image for a second of an alternative story, where the differences between us were diminished and where when I spoke to her, it was in Gujarati.

QUIET REBEL

Caryn Solomon

South Africa – England

"When we talk about our mothers we witness a life, but when we narrow it to our drama, we deliver incomplete portrayals."

Ellen Vrana. The Examined Life

Writing about my mother, I wonder whose story I'm telling.

Whatever I write, it's my version of *her* past, but also of *ours*, shared from the day I was born – even before. Where would our stories intersect – and how? Telling her own version, she'd tell of other pasts. How do I capture and tell *her* life?

Time has favoured this moment. At 92 she's still here, all there and eager to share, to add her voice to the telling, not just her words but also her cadence and language and turn of phrase.

Still, when it comes to the writing, I'm stuck. Which voice do I use – first-person autobiography as told to me, or third-person biography? Do I transcribe and copy it all verbatim, or pick and choose, distil the essence of it? How do I show her mobile, fleeting expressions, her twinkles and frowns, her gaze – sometimes right 'here', sometimes out 'there', where she goes to remember.

She talks and talks and gives me her personal diaries, written seventy years ago, together with her permission to write whatever I wish, to share whatever I think I know, to say what I feel. Still, I worry. Is this story true and fair? Have I exposed too much?

Along the way, I send her drafts to critique (after all, she taught literature for more than forty years). She always comes back with encouraging, useful suggestions – a bit more of this, a bit less of that. Mostly she's happy with how it's evolving. But still I worry.

"Mom, are you sure it's OK for me to write about that – the way *I* saw it?"

"Oh yes, sweetheart – absolutely sure."

"You don't mind that my story is sometimes different from yours?"

"No, not all – I simply take it as a piece of writing"

So here we are.

2019

My mother and I are sitting at the African yellowwood table that came from Johannesburg to Bristol forty years ago. These half-drunk mugs of warm tea – Earl Grey for her, Rooibos for me – know exactly where they belong on this honey-coloured slab of wood that has listened to our stories, weathered our conflicts, embraced our secrets ever since I'd slouch in from school, plonk myself down at one end and mom would say, "I don't suppose you'd like a cup of tea, darling."

The cast-iron wood-burning stove, comfortably tucked into the flag-stone Georgian hearth behind me looks quaint and romantic, like something from Hansel and Gretel. Nothing like that in our airy, white-tiled kitchen in Africa, it's still quite a novelty to me, even now after all these years. But Julia Isaacs, my mother's grandmother, would no doubt have warmed her chilblains at one quite similar in the sooty kitchen of her mother's boarding house in Whitechapel.

A plate of shortbread biscuits rests untouched next to the mugs.

"Have one darling. I feel so bad, I didn't make lunch for you."

"No thanks Mom. It's fine – I'm not at all hungry."

"I wanted to have something nice waiting for you."

"Mom, please don't worry – I'm fine. Really."

"OK then – I'm ready."

I press the video button on my iPhone.

"So tell me, Mom, what do you remember?"

Joan:

I'm lying down with my mother Rose in the back bedroom. We're on the bed opposite the window. It's as sunny as all hell outside but she's wearing a warm woollen dress. I am stroking her back. She is asleep. That is my earliest memory.

My second memory is my father painting the skirting board. A tin of paint stands open, half full. I am wondering what will happen if I kick it. So I kick it. My father stands up – a big man to me. He puts his hand in his pocket and takes out a penny. 'Go buy some sweets with your mother and leave me alone.'

But what I love to remember the most is making mud-pies, sucking flowers from the honeysuckle hedge, walking from school stealing handfuls of petals from roses to press on my nails, making them red.

Wait! I know this child – she is the one who played with *me!*

Child-mother of my childhood – loving, curious, brave, spirited, playful, inventive. And here she is now, in these word-droplets of time past, spilling into the air between us, drinking tea at the kitchen table. This is the sap of her that has given me life, all my life.

"How old were you then, Mom?"

"Lying with my mother and kicking the tin, about three. When I stole the petals, already at school."

"And you still remember it all clearly?"

"Yes. Perfectly clearly."

Today, at ninety-two, her voice trembles, her speech has slowed, she's frustrated at having 'lost the words I need to express what I'm thinking', but remembering what she remembers, her energy simmers, fuelling a purpose I cannot name. I sense her impatience to tell it – again and again.

"Mom, do you remember, you showed me how to colour my nails with petals too?"

"Yes I do – and so many other things too we did together."

And then we are talking about 'the time we swam in the sea in the storm'.

My mother and I. Running across the empty beach, white sand stippled by stabbing drops of warm rain, the sky belching purple and black, roiling thunder, electric crackle of light – sheets and flashes of it – we dash, stride, jump and fling ourselves through waves exquisite as laced marble and Chinese jade, raging and crashing, this is the mighty Atlantic rearing, dangerous-high and foaming-cruel – this is a storm on its way!

Dad, from the shore, already dressed, is waving and calling, "We have to get off this beach before the lightning strikes."

Tossing backwards over the tops of the waves, faces raised to the sky, mouths open to drink the rain, grabbing each other's outstretched hands, Mom and I are dancing. Gulping, gasping, nothing to stand on, gouging our eyes with our fists to clear them of salt and sting, exhausted from laughing and bashing around, we fight our way through the backwash, reaching shoreward. Collapsed on the sand, we count the seconds from flash to boom – the storm is near, there's just enough time to inhale and whoop with each clap of thunder.

We run up the beach, slapping bare feet, now almost numb from being in the water so long, imprint our tracks on the hard, wet sand, which instantly sucks up all trace of us.

Halfway along, we stop, as if to the beat of a cosmic gong.

Dad and Ryan are moving towards the dunes – the rain is taking a breath.

We turn to look at each other.

"What are we doing?" she laughs.

As one, we spin and run, as if for our lives, back to the waves.

* * *

Here in the kitchen, it's peaceful and calm, but the moment vibrates – my pounding heart seems to be giving birth to the flush on my mother's cheeks.

"Mom, why do we love remembering that so much?"

"We had the whole sea to ourselves. It was much too stormy for anyone else to take that risk. And now, what else do you want to know?"

"Tell me about Granny Rose and Grandpa Phil."

Rose and Phil

Sauntering jauntily down Adderley Street that sunny afternoon past Stuttafords' windows, enjoying the reflection of his own good looks, you'd never have guessed he was 'on the run from the coppers' – a fugitive, just returned to South Africa – wanted in Rhodesia for assaulting a man who'd called him 'a bloody Jew'. Phillip Mendelsohn, my mother's father, son of poor Latvian Jews who'd escaped to South Africa in the late 1800s, fleeing pogroms in Eastern Europe.

Born on a train from Cape Town to Johannesburg, Phil left school at twelve to take a job at the Empire cinema, winding films. A few years later, he became an apprentice compositor, arranging movable type for the daily papers.

At seventeen, newly qualified, he set off to explore the world beyond South Africa's borders. Fearless, inventive, curious, smart, he soon involved himself in various 'schemes' to make money. Farming tobacco in Rhodesia had seemed like a good idea.

Throughout his life, his optimism seldom waned, but he never became a wealthy man.

* * *

That same afternoon, as she knelt on the floor pinning a mannequin in Stuttafords' largest street-facing window, Rose Isaacs, lithe, slender, with clear blue eyes and long red hair, caught sight of a "dashing young man in a white linen suit and Panama hat" staring directly at her "through the winda". His eyebrows were fierce but his eyes were warm. Lifting his right arm, he balanced his thumb on his nose, opened his palm and wiggled his hand. She wiggled hers back. He held up five fingers and arched his brows.

She nodded. At 5 o'clock precisely, she walked outside to where he was waiting. They went for an ice cream.

* * *

Despite being born and raised in Cape Town, my grandmother Rose always referred to London as "home" and spoke with the same Cockney accent as her five older siblings born in Whitechapel, London. Six more brothers and sisters would follow – in all, the Isaacs siblings were six boys and six girls.

Telling stories of home, Rosie would straighten her back and raise her head with pride, especially describing her father Judah Isaacs's shoulders, shoulders so strong that at thirteen years old he could haul great wooden pallets of fresh fish on his own through Billingsgate market, to "make a few shillins". But truth be told, she had no real sense of her working-class Jewish family's modest beginnings in the East End of London, from which few roads led out and upwards, nor of their daily struggle to make ends meet, selling pencils and second-hand clothes in Petticoat Lane.

Thanks to the fortune made by her father's cousins, Harry and Barnett Isaacs, Rose and her siblings were raised on the lower slopes of Table Mountain, in a lavish mansion behind the Mount Nelson Hotel, in Cape Town. With seven servants, a ballroom, smoking room and clothes shipped from Europe – "button-down boots from Paris, we Isaacs girls were the first in Cape Town to wear 'em" – Rose remained blissfully unaware of her privilege.

Unlike her six brothers, boisterous lads who were free to spread their wings, Rose and her sisters were strictly forbidden from stepping beyond the garden gate on their own. And for Rose herself, "The Barratt of Wimpole Street" (her name for her father) had a plan: to marry his daughter off to the heir to the Toblerone chocolate fortune – a "good *khap*" (good catch) whose own father was Judah's friend.

But red-headed Rosie, fearless and headstrong, had plans of her own. Donning a pair of trousers ("unthinkable!"), she jumped the garden gate, and ("horror of horrors!") took a job dressing windows for Stuttafords, Cape Town's largest department store.

Judah never forgave his daughter for picking a hot-tempered, penniless adventurer instead of the match he'd arranged.

* * *

Rose's mother, Julia Isaacs (nee Hart), was also from London's East End. But, unlike her husband, Judah's fair-skinned, blue-eyed family, she was olive-skinned with curly hair and sad brown eyes. Her forebears were Mendozas, Sephardic Jews expelled from Spain and Portugal at the end of the fifteenth century, during the Inquisition, finally landing in England, during the 1700s.

Joan

My mother Rose only remembered her own mother, Julia, being pregnant. She had eighteen confinements. Maybe her mother was a good mother, but they were never close.

When Julia sailed back to England to visit her relatives, Rose went to live with her African nanny's family out on the farm in the African bush. She stayed there for five months, sleeping in a hut with all the children tumbled together on mud floors.

She loved being with them so much she didn't want to leave.

She always said it was the happiest time of her childhood – her only memory of anyone mothering her.

After losing six newborns and raising twelve children, Julia died at sixty-four. I never heard a single story from Rose or anyone else in the family about anything Julia said and whenever they spoke about her, they called her "poor Ma"!

* * *

One of Rose's most treasured possessions was a hand-written letter with a large golden stamp on the front. It came from "the Queen 'erself," congratulating Rose and Phil on their sixtieth wedding anniversary. In all, they were married for seventy years.

When she was nearly eighty, I asked her what she loved most about being a woman.

"Putting on lipstick, spraying perfume – *4711* – making myself beautiful for my 'usband."

"What can you tell me about keeping a marriage together?"

"Phil's a difficult man, a man with a temper. When he shouts I keep quiet – let him get it out of his system. When he's done, I smile and say, 'Phil darlin', would you like a cuppa tea?'"

"And what about sex?"

"I closed my eyes and thought about England and what to make for supper."

My granny Rose died in our arms, my mother's and mine. She was holding my hand. Her last words to me were: "Tell Nina (my daughter) not to get married and waste her life on a man." She was ninety-five.

The day after she died, Phil climbed into bed, refused to eat and started to shout, over and over, "Where's my Rosie? I want my bloody wife!" Still healthy and strong, he took five full days to will himself to death. He was ninety-six.

* * *

Newly married, Rose and Phil lived in a one-roomed flat on the top floor of a block in Eloff Street, the main street in downtown Johannesburg. Phil made tables, chairs and shelves from old wooden fruit crates. Rosie made costumes for the ballet and hats for special occasions. They went to parties every week.

Phil went to work setting type for the papers, working giant hot metal presses. Rosie would speak with pride of his never being afraid to do a "job which blackened 'is 'ands". During World War II, when indelible ink became scarce, he'd be out of work. Never one to be a victim, Rosie would support herself, Phil and their two daughters with her sewing.

Hard-working and eager to start a family, after four years in Eloff Street, they had saved enough to move to Yeoville, originally proclaimed as a suburb in 1890, four years after the discovery of gold led to the founding of Johannesburg.

Perched on a ridge overlooking the dirty, smoke-filled gold-mining town that had sprung from the desolate scrub of the Transvaal bushveld, Yeoville was advertised as a 'sanitarium for the rich' where the air was pure and trees grew.

But the rich did not buy into the marketing hype and Yeoville became a multiclass area, attracting waves of immigrants from around the world, seeking a better life.

It was there that my mother and her sister were born in a modest, four-roomed house with a red-polished *stoep,* a back garden, with trees – plum and fig – and a thick, green lawn of coarse African Kikuyu grass.

Home

Sarah Joan, my mother, only ever known as Joan, was born on the 26th of November, 1927. You could guess from her olive skin, deep brown eyes and her mop of dark curls that her forebears might have come from Spain.

Two years later, her sister Babette arrived, pearly-skinned, hazel-eyed, with Rose's red hair – an Isaacs through and through.

They both inherited the strong 'Isaacs chin', their mother's lithe frame and masses of hair; soon they'd be known as 'the Mendelsohn girls' with 'plaits down to their knees'.

Joan

Every night my mother, Babette and I waited for my father to come home from work. After a glass of milk and a bath, he would sit on the 'stoep' in the Morris chair with my sister on one side and me on the other. He didn't have a chance to read the paper he'd opened between us.

After dinner, we'd sit together to listen to the radio or play Monopoly. My dad cheated like hell – he paid us out with our own money.

But what I really loved was to sit on the back lawn with Jack, sharing his stew with 'mealie meal' and gravy. Jack came to us when I was three months old, looking for 'housework'. A young Shangaan boy – eighteen years at the most – he'd come from Letaba, a bush village up near the Kruger Park. By the time he left us, more than forty years later, he was old and grey.

Every night, after he'd eaten, he'd play the pop-pop. That's what I called it. It looked like a bow. Keeping one end in his mouth he'd hum and pluck the string to make music. I'd sit beside him, lost in the rhythm and sound.

Jack gave me his food, his music, his stories, his love and protection – he was my bond with Africa and, even today, hearing African music tugs at my heart like nothing else.

Even now I can see the bow at the back of his apron. He always put me behind his back when my mother was cross with me. I think I loved him more than my own parents.

My mother also loved him – she taught him everything she knew – and everything he did, he did to perfection. He was her true companion.

Every afternoon I walked with him to the dairy. One day, on our way home, the police stopped us.

"Waar's jou pas?" ("Where's your passbook?" – permit for 'non-whites' to live and work in the cities during Apartheid.)

My mother came out to the street.

"Leave him alone. He works here. If you don't go, you'll be sorry."
So they left him alone.

Being black in South Africa – I didn't realize what it was really like. I wasn't aware that things were abnormal – black and white people living apart from each other – whites 'here', blacks 'there' (unless they had permits to be domestic workers). To be honest, I never wondered why there were no black children at my school. Why would I?

Mahlambane (Jack's little girl) stayed with us too and slept with me in my bedroom. I came home from school and bathed her every day. I taught her to knit and sew, write and read. I loved that child to distraction.

When she left us to go to school in her village, I sat on the pavement, crying and crying. For three days I refused to go to school. She was seven, I was thirteen.

* * *

Weekends, Uncle Morrie would come. A gentle lovely man who worked at Wings – a gentleman's outfitting store.

He always brought a bag of sweets – every time, the same sweets. He and I would sit and listen to the symphony concert on the radio, while my parents slept and my sister went out on her bike with Morris Klass. I was very, very jealous. My mother wouldn't let me ride a bike in case it damaged my feet for dancing.

At fourteen, I had my first date. With Uncle Morrie. I took the tram to where he was waiting to take me to see Madame Butterfly with a little box of chocolates. We sat in the stalls. It was the first time I'd seen an opera not from the wings. That would become a life-long love affair, me and opera.

Outside, the day has surrendered to grey and the rain of a murky November. But here in the old Georgian kitchen, suffused with the light of re-living, my mother's face is that of a child in the African sun. Now she is looking right through me, eyes dusky, pulling me into her story.

I wonder why she's chosen *these* snippets to tell about 'home' – there are so many stories I've heard from her and from others more exciting, dramatic, momentous – but it's *these* she wants to remember most, to enliven her sense, and mine, of what really mattered and who she was then – perhaps of who she still is and wants to be, now.

Joan

And now I remember swinging on the gate in front of our house. My mother is chatting to Mrs. Schuman over the fence. Good friends and neighbours they were.

One day, the Schumans' relatives came to visit. Hearing their Yiddish accents, Rose said they were all 'Peruvians'. After that she stopped talking to the Schumans altogether. In so many ways, kindness was my mother's second name. But when it came to 'foreign' Jews, she was an inveterate snob.

My mother's judgment feels like a slap. She waits, to see what I'll say.
"Wow, Mom, that's harsh."
"Maybe so, but she was."
I push my chair back and march to the kettle.
"More tea?"
"Earl Grey, black please. And I need a break."
Good. She's given me time to gather my thoughts.

* * *

My adored Granny Rosie. For me, she was all blue eyes and making things – pictures and tutus, soup with saffron, coconut ice and baked custard, cardboard houses with cellophane windows (red, blue and yellow), stories of clocks that spoke, white cloth napkins draped round her fist into puppets of kittens and puppies meowing and yapping, doodles that morphed into faces and flowers, arguments short on reason, long on rapture and silky-slidey songs:

> *"The mooooon has his eyes on youuuu.*
> *So be careful of what you dooooo.*
> *Every time you go a-strollin' with your lady-love.*
> *Mister moon is watchin' from above..."*

And, my favourite...

> *"A song of love is a saaaad song.*
> *Hi-Lili, Hi-Lili, Hi-Lo*
> *A song of love is a song of woe.*
> *Don't ask me how I know..."*

Which is why I always called her Granny Hi-Lili.

Knitting shawls and socks, making bread and oxtail stew for the cold and hungry, unconcerned about race, colour, class or creed, she always would stop to save every lame duck that crossed her path, her open heart a well of loving-kindness.

But maybe my mother was right. Until she died in her nineties, I barely heard from Rosie an unkind word about anyone – except a certain group who lived in the five-star retirement home in Johannesburg where she and Phil ended their days – a few frail, elderly women, Yiddish speakers. They too she called 'Peruvians'. She never knew the true meaning of the word, but for her it was reason enough to avoid the communal dining room and Sunday evening films.

Peruvians

Jews in England

"Mrs. Isaacs and Mrs. Jacobs rarely quarrelled with each other, uniting rather in opposition to the rest of the Square. They were English, quite English…and they gave themselves airs in consequence and called their kinder 'children', which annoyed those neighbours who found a larger admixture of Yiddish necessary for conversation. These very kinder, again, attained considerable importance among their schoolfellows by refusing to pronounce the guttural 'ch' of Hebrew otherwise than as an English 'k'."
(Children of the Ghetto by Israel Zangwill, 1892)

'Mrs. Isaacs' wasn't Rosie. But, listening to her views on Yiddish, she certainly could have been.

I want to know why my all-loving granny Rose was so intolerant of a people she had barely encountered face to face. Something tells me I have to go back to England and sleuth backwards in time to find out.

* * *

Before I know it, it's 1066.

King William the Conqueror brings a group of Jewish merchants from Rouen to England and gives them special status as 'property of the King', outside of the feudal system. Why? Jews are good at trade. Their commercial skills and capital will make England more prosperous. But, there are conditions: they are not permitted to own land or participate in any trade on their own behalf (except medicine). Instead, they are forced to take up jobs prohibited for Christians: collecting tax for the Crown, rent on behalf of baron landlords and lending money for interest. Of all debt collected by Jews, ten percent goes to the King. Many Christians become indebted to Jewish moneylenders.

King Henry I, happy to see how Jews help to expand the royal coffers, grants them a royal charter allowing them to move about the country without paying tolls, to buy and sell goods, to sell their pledges, to be tried in court by their peers and to swear oaths on the Jewish bible.

Under Henry II, with economic expansion and increased demand for credit, Jews enjoy a short 'golden age' until 1189. But from then on, Anglo-Jewish history until the 19th century becomes a litany of mob violence, seizing of assets, forced segregation, massacres, burnings, hangings, imprisonments, the spread of the Blood Libel (Jews accused of murdering Christian children to drink their blood) and Crusades enforcing conversion.

In the eyes of Christians, Jews are greedy, malevolent, merciless demons taking money, poisoning wells, twisting minds, killing children and selling Christian souls and bodies.

1290: King Edward I expels all Jews from England. They're allowed to take only what they can carry.

For the next three hundred and sixty-six years, the only 'Jews' in England are 'conversos', originally from Spain and Portugal, forced, during the Inquisition, to choose between Christian baptism and execution. Many have continued to practise their religion in secret.

Among these are my great-grandmother Julia's Sephardic ancestors – hiding in England under the guise of 'conversion'. Their survival relies on remaining unseen.

1656: Oliver Cromwell allows Jews to return to England. But though Jewish people have disappeared for nearly four hundred years, anti-Judaism has not. Harassment, anti-Semitic attacks and prescriptions on trade, dress, where to bury their dead and more, continue.

Nevertheless, Jews do well – well enough to finance Wellington through the Napoleonic wars, the British government's purchase of Egypt's interest in the Suez Canal and Cecil John Rhodes' development of the British South Africa Company.

1858: The Emancipation of Jews is declared – seven hundred and ninety-two years after Jews first set foot on English soil.

* * *

In the East End of London, life for most English Jews has never been easy, but some are beginning to prosper as small shopkeepers. Among these is the Isaacs family, settled in England since the 1700s.

At twelve years old, having mastered the basics of numeracy and literacy, Rose's father, Judah Isaacs, slightly built, but wiry and strong, becomes a fish porter at London's Billingsgate fish market. It's a coveted job which earns more money in less time than any other unskilled labour in Europe – you can earn twenty shillings a day, being finished by 10 am, hauling trunks of fish, balanced on your head, from the ships in the dock up to one of the 140 stands selling fish at auction.

At fifteen, Judah marries Julia Hart, also fifteen. During the following twelve years, they will bear eight children. Three will be lost and life in London will be a struggle to make ends meet.

Jews arrive from Eastern Europe
'Whitechapel has never recovered from the overcrowding that arose when, night after night, wagon-loads of poor Jews were brought up from the docks, where they had just arrived, still panic-stricken, from Russia.' (The Lancet, 1884.)

One and a half thousand miles eastwards, within the Russian Empire, Jews have not been as lucky. Forced to live in the Pale of Settlement, a massive western region of Imperial Russia, excluded from land ownership, education and public service, most Jews are working as artisans in *shtetls* (small villages). Jewish culture is kept alive by their language, Yiddish, a mixture of German and Hebrew, and intellectual life is fed by *yeshivas* (religious schools), where learning is underpinned by question and debate. But life is hard and impoverished, many cannot put food on the table and always the threat of anti-Semitism looms, increasingly erupting in violent *pogroms* (anti-Jewish riots).

Between 1880 and 1914, no fewer than two million Jews flee to America, Canada, Argentina, France, South Africa and 150,000 come to Britain. On wagons, trains and boats, their possessions are few and their bags light, but wherever they go they carry with them their faith and their language.

Wretchedly poor and traumatised, the newly arrived Jews are different and strange. Their poverty, menial occupations and foreignness draw hostile attention to them and to English-born Jews alike, fuelling fires of xenophobia and anti-Semitism.

The *olive-skinned women* and 'dark-bearded men' in Russian-Polish dress are *not European or, at all events, not English*; their religious customs, with prayers chanted in a *nasal, snuffling tone*, *wild ejaculations which taper into growling murmurs*, *muttering* and *half-singing, half-talking... forming a chaos of uncouth sound*, are *not consonant with our notions of reverence and religious propriety*. (*The Times*, reporting on the reopening of the Great Synagogue in Duke's Palace, London, September 1852).

Equally puzzling is Yiddish, their language, which most of all begins to define the area as 'Jewish'. Shopkeepers with unpronounceable names sell goods advertised in an incomprehensible language, locals gabble in an unknown tongue. Speaking only Yiddish, the newcomers cannot communicate with or work for Gentiles and, being religious, they cannot work on the Sabbath (sundown on Friday to sundown on Saturday).

Gradually, they spread into whole districts formerly outside the Jewish quarter. Amongst the non-Jewish locals living amongst them, their alien presence arouses long-held hatreds and many grievances, at the heart of which lies one thing only: the immigrants are not English:

"The prejudiced Englishman is apt to call 'dirty' whatever is foreign." (Canon A.S. Barnett, warden of the Whitechapel settlement of Toynbee Hall)

Anglo-Jews, like the Isaacs family, whose roots in the country are generations deep, have assumed that political emancipation has resolved Jewish status. But a mass influx of foreign Jews with indecent, un-English customs, superstition, dirt and clannishness is a threat to their English compatriots' position and wellbeing.

The reactions of Anglo-Jews vary in intensity and kind. Mostly sympathetic to the sufferings of Jews under tsarist rule, they try to help. But, some, more well-to-do, actively discourage this 'race of strangers' from staying in England at all, going as far as paying for their passage back home to Eastern Europe and other parts of the world.

By the turn of the century, the flood of impoverished foreign Jews into one small area is seen as part of a social crisis affecting the whole of London. Within a short time, social investigators are organising enquiries into the 'Jewish Question'. Social and religious reformers are introducing 'remedies', including creating a cadre of Yiddish speaking constables, better to arrest Jewish wrongdoers. Jew-baiting and Jew-beatings by locals are not uncommon and no one makes a distinction between English and foreign Jew.

'As long as there is a section of Jews in England who proclaim themselves aliens by their mode of life, by their very looks, by every word they utter, so long will the entire community bean object of distrust to Englishmen' (Jewish Chronicle, *7 August 1901*)

The Isaacs family leaves

Six thousand miles south, Judah's Isaacs's cousin, Barnett, is now one of the richest men in the world.

At thirteen years old, he and his older brother Harry had left the Jews' Free School in London where, in addition to Hebrew, they had learned reading and writing in English, as well as enough arithmetic to help in their father Isaac Isaacs's Petticoat Lane shop selling second-hand clothes. At night the brothers earned pennies as boxers, touts and performers in London's East End music halls, where songs were sung in Yiddish.

By 1873, after changing their names to 'something more Italian' in order to attract audiences to their music hall acts, the 'Barnato Brothers' had saved enough for one-way tickets to sail to South Africa to join the diamond rush. There, having arrived with little more than a box of cigars and the shirts on their backs, they have made their fortunes as entrepreneurs in diamonds and gold.

In addition to building schools, synagogues and civic centres, supporting the South African Jewish press and helping to relocate refugees from Eastern Europe, Barnett (now famously known as Barney Barnato) has never forgotten his humble beginnings and will also help to pave the way to a better life for relatives left behind in London, including his cousin Judah's family, caught in the slipstream of vicious, age-old, anti-Semitic prejudice, reignited by the arrival of 'foreigners' who threaten the still-fragile status and safety of English Jews.

* * *

When Judah and Julia Isaacs board a steamer at Southampton bound for Cape Town, they have in tow five children, six brown leather trunks of varying sizes filled with all their worldly possessions and food for the journey in canvas bags.

I wonder what they are thinking and feeling, standing on deck, watching England grow smaller and smaller. Perhaps they are silent, taking one last look; perhaps there are tears – of wrenching sadness, knowing how unlikely they are to return, or relief to be leaving behind the daily grind of making a living. Perhaps they're afraid, of falling sick and of what they don't know. Perhaps they are crying and laughing at once, excited to make a new start. Perhaps, like the slaves from Egypt, they are filled with hope for the Promised Land.

Of course I'll never know, but the echo resounding for me through their story is this: stowed beneath the inevitable sadness, excitement, fear and hope, is the unfinished business – deep, rage-inducing guilt. Walking away from desperate humans seeking help is not easy for kind people who know what it means to be hounded. But what choice do you feel you have when, after literally hundreds of years of persecution, their invasion of 'your space', their very existence, threatens yours?

* * *

Two years after the Isaacs family lands in Cape Town, Rose arrives, the first of Judah and Julia's children to be born in South Africa. The year is 1897.

* * *

I was always aware when she spoke, that granny Rose sounded different. Not only her accent, but also her turn of phrase. Having spent my early childhood years in London, I myself was used to people who sounded like her, but no one I knew in South Africa dropped their 'h's' or said "bloomin'" or "bloomers" or "jam roly-poly".

After years listening to Rose's stories about her life, I began to realize why she spoke as she did: she may have been born in Africa, but she learned how to speak from parents and older siblings who spoke like the East London Jews that they were.

And what did they talk about, night after night, at the long, mahogany table, eating their English dinner of mashed potatoes, peas, carrots, fried fish or roast chicken and a 'nice baked dish for pudding'? Like most Jewish families I'm sure they told stories. And what were those stories about? Like most migrant families, I'm sure they told stories of 'home'.

From the time she could understand words, perhaps even before, imbibing the 'sense of it', granny Rose would have listened to stories of what had been left behind, witnessed the pull of home remembered, the grieving for home lost. Hearing her parents' and siblings' stories told and retold, stories of dislocation and loss, she too would have felt their rage – rage towards those who had crashed into the only place where the Isaacs family, for more than a hundred years, had felt safe – rage towards those loud, religious, filthy, foreign, Yiddish speaking invaders – in short, Peruvians.

For the rest of her life, Rose would, in their presence, migrate *herself*. In my mother's terms, behave just like an 'inveterate snob'.

* * *

This was all before my mother was born and raised in a country where all the darkest forces of hate of the 'other' were directed at those with 'non-white' skins. Jew-hatred also lived in the hearts and minds of white, Nazi-supporting Calvinists running the country, but, alongside Zulus, Xhosas, Tswanas, Shangaans, Swazis, Pedis, Sothos and many more, a few hundred thousand Jews were small fry.

My mother, a white Jewish woman, was, in South Africa, ironically spared by the colour of her skin. But she was all too aware of what it meant to be on the losing side. To her, being born on the winning side would become a call to battle – a call to defend those South Africans brutally oppressed by a vicious White Supremacist regime.

No matter how unconscious, unwitting or ignorant, no racial insult would ever escape her ire. Race hatred was race hatred: brown, pink or Peruvian.

Dancing

Joan
Dancing in the kitchen…dancing in the kitchen… my shoes off. I tried it the other day. I couldn't stay upright, never mind bend to take off my shoes.

There are hundreds of things I can't do anymore. Nobody knows the struggle I have every day – I don't look ninety-two.

But dancing – I loved it beyond everything. Exercising my body. Mastering the technique. Being able to do it without thinking.

My dancing was my mother's life. She'd seen Pavlova when she was young. More than anything, she wanted me to be a dancer like that. In her mind I was. Ha! I was far from being Pavlova, believe me! But she was happy and utterly dedicated. I can still picture her running in front of me – her little bandy legs running for the tram, to take me to dancing.

When I gave it up, she was heartbroken. So was I. But I wanted more. I had to make a choice – dancing or university. I couldn't keep trying to write my essays in the dressing room in between making up.

Casting my inner gaze across the span of our shared lifetimes, I catch my breath. Walking, running, sitting, gardening, reading, riding her bike, swimming, painting, waving her arms in delight, frustration, farewell, even standing still my mother seems to be moving, stepping on air, a leaf on a breeze.

And now I'm back in our Jo'burg kitchen, perched on the edge of this very same table. Granny Hi-Lilli has said it's bad luck to sit on a table – no one will want to marry me. But I don't care about that – I'm only ten and I'm here to watch my mother dance.

The music begins. She's the only one who can hear it, but I know it's Tchaikovsky, inside her head.

Slowly she starts to waft in circles, rising and sinking and rising again in a spiral, weaving invisible patterns. Her outstretched arms are wings – perhaps she's a bird, longing to fly – or a flower with tendrils stretching for something just out of reach.

And then she's off, stretching and spilling, hair tumbling, face alive with the music, leaping around the kitchen as if it were sky, arms and legs setting her fingers and toes alight, telling an epic story, falling and rising, peeling her feet off the floor, she's running away but it looks like she wants to be caught – a nymph, purposely tripping.

Slowing down to a standstill, her body is strong, like a statue, but supple and soft, like a body.

Her back dead-straight, slowly she lifts and stretches one leg behind her, fanning it up in an arc to the ceiling. Her standing leg is a pole holding her whole weight. That single foot is so brave! Leaning forward, head up, her arms reach out and open to form a sideways 'V' – a perfect arabesque. For just one instant she turns her head to the side and throws me a fleeting smile – sheer pleasure mixed with something that looks like triumph.

Beyond the slanted horizon which runs through her chest from fingers to toes, I can see the trees through the window, outside in our garden, wildly waving from side to side. I know it's only an afternoon summer storm on its way, but it feels like the day is lifting its skirts to join the dance.

* * *

Nearly sixty years on, much has faded, but the light of remembrance carries on shining on what I loved most – her beauty, grace, passion, sheer *joie de vivre* and explosive abandon – magic that moved things and turned the world upside down.

Still slim, her back is not quite as straight and her turned-out feet have begun to falter. Seeing her delicate frame, graceful as ever, neatly tucked and curved into the spindle back of the kitchen chair, bony fingers curled round that half-full mug, her walking stick just within reach, brings tears to my eyes.

But hers are knowing and bright and her hair, carefully draped in that old, familiar tortoiseshell clip, still spills and flows, as does her dancing spirit.

My mother may have left dancing but dancing never left her.

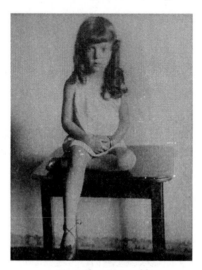

Joan, three years old

Of course, I went to ballet class too. But my musical talent wasn't enough to point my pigeon toes out in the right direction, or to rescue my dangling tangle of too-long, skinny arms.

When my teacher gently suggested I give up dancing and stick with piano instead, my mother seemed not to mind. But *I* felt I'd let her down.

When Nina, my daughter, arrived with the dancing gene, I was delighted. She would be my mother's reincarnation. But when, after a year or two of weekly lessons, Nina said, 'I want to do ballet for you, but not for me,' I knew she'd been sent to teach me, not to be my absolution.

Quiet rebel

Joan

Every Sunday morning, my father washed my hair. It was down to my knees. While it was drying, we made ice cream.

At eighteen, I was sick of it. But no one dared to cut it. My cousin found me someone who would – a barber who begged me to take it home in a bag, but I threw it all away in his bin. After I left, he fished it out, made four switches and sold them.

All my life I didn't do the conventional thing.

Stuffing her shorn hair into her beret, my mother dragged herself home, arriving just in time for dinner – Rose's English stew, roast potatoes, baked apples and custard. The beret remained in place.

Dinner was always a lively affair – everyone had a story to tell: Madame Poppy Frames, *grande dame* of ballet, ferocious and feared, whipping her pupils' ankles, her little stick barely distinct from her skeletal fingers; Babette's latest medal for backstroke; the Peruvniks next door cooking tripe, the SMELL, what next?

Rose, as always, would hold the floor with her comic asides and malapropisms.

"I know we all 'ave our little syncrasies, but those foreigners – look what they eat!"

Phil's attention was elsewhere, "Why don't you take off your beret?"

From across the table, my mother's doleful eyes fixed themselves on the wall behind her father's head. She dragged the beret sideways, releasing a few curls which barely touched her shoulders.

Suddenly pale, Phil stared for a second, stood, turned, walked out. No one spoke.

* * *

Why mom, why did you do it – break the heart of your mother's dreams for you, chop off your father's pride and joy and literally chuck it away? Were you feeling courageous? Or angry? Or simply trapped by being 'for them' and not 'for you'?

Rose was born in an era when marriage was really the end of the road. By the time you arrived, she would have felt she'd already accomplished everything she would ever accomplish. You – physical, clever, artistic, her talents reborn – were supposed to stoke the fire of her dreams, to dance her unfulfilled life.

But you carried an untamed spark, 'the unconventional thing', a spark which would burn a new path, a path which would take the rest of your life to travel.

Boys

Joan

Before we were seventeen, we never had real boyfriends.

Oh yes, loads of boys were after me, but mostly I wasn't interested. They called me a can of peaches – sweet inside but tough to open. That's how I liked it.

Except Lionel Mazebow – he wasn't my boyfriend, but boy could he dance! I loved to go dancing with him. But that was all.

Then there was Raymond Shapiro – he was my boyfriend.

Drum major and rugby star, his school wanted to keep him there as long as possible. That wouldn't have been hard – he was as thick as two planks. I had to write his essays to get him through Matric. But he was sweet and very good-looking. Every week I went to watch him play. No wonder I don't like rugby now.

After two years together, he asked me to marry him. I was nineteen! I didn't want to marry ANYONE!

Phillip Stein and Jerry Shaper and Lyn Gillis also wanted to marry me. I had to get away. I phoned my cousin Fay Hummel to ask if I could spend my university holiday with her. "No boys to bother me in Upington," I thought – "it's the Kalahari desert."

I went for three weeks. Three days before I left to come home, I met a young man who looked more like a boy, too young to be at medical school. He was different from all the others. He wanted to talk about Chaucer and asked if he could hold my hand.

Louis Solomon. Playful, earnest, boyish, nineteen years old, his slim frame and fine-featured, soulful face were unlike most of the other white people who lived in that dusty bushveld farming community on the banks of the Orange River. They were Afrikaners, tall, big-boned, tough, hardy, weather-beaten frontier people, descendants of Dutch and French Hugue-nots, strict Protestants who had settled in the Cape Colony in 1652.

But here too was a small community of Jewish families who had fled Eastern Europe at the turn of the century. At first, many were *smouses* (itin-erant pedlars) travelling the *veld* (countryside) on donkey carts filled with small household goods. Now there were doctors, dentists, small business owners and farmers growing and trading fruit and lucerne (cattle feed). As well as English and, in some cases, Yiddish, they all spoke fluent Afrikaans.

Each December, at the end of the academic year, Louis would board a train in Cape Town to take the two-day journey north to Upington, a dusty outback town on the edge of the Kalahari Desert. From there, a twenty-six-mile donkey-cart ride to Keimoes, a hamlet too small to be on the map, where Solly, Louis' father and Louis Miller, his uncle, owned Solomon and Miller, the only general goods store for miles. There, Louis would spend three blissful weeks with his cousins and friends reliving his barefoot Kalahari childhood.

The highlight of 'varsity vac' was the end-of-holidays, all-day picnic on the banks of the Orange River – a feast of freshly-picked salads and fruit, *braaied* (barbecued) jacket potatoes, *mielies* (corn on the cob), chicken and *boerewors* (farmer's sausage seasoned with ground coriander, pepper, nutmeg and allspice), home-made bread, rusks for dipping in hot, sweet, milky tea and *melktert* (custard tart) freshly baked by 'the best baker for miles', Anne Solomon, Louis' mother.

The afternoon would be spent strolling alongside the pebbled shore of the river or perched on water-smoothed rocks, chatting and laughing, then curling up for a nap on a bed of dry grasses, mindful of thorns, snakes, sharp stones and the blistering sun.

In December 1948, the Hummels' cousin from Jo'burg was amongst the young students gathered there – a large-eyed, olive-skinned beauty, graceful as a swan.

Joan
I knew straight away. No hesitation. In fact, there was hesitation. I wrote to my sister the night I met him to tell her "I've found a very nice boy for you." By the morning I'd changed my mind – I'd keep him for myself.

I never did a wiser thing in my life.

Daddy didn't exactly propose. He just said: "Our children will have to be bilingual." And I said, "Yes." Three days after we met, we were engaged.

Joan and Louis on the banks of the Orange River, 1948.

* * *

Some of my very early childhood lessons on love took place late at night, lying awake in bed. From the quiet dark of my bedroom, I could hear the deepening rumble of water filling their bath. A moment of silence, faint whoosh and ripple as they climbed in and sat down together and then, for hours, their hushed talk – night after night – together in the bath.

Some lessons also took place during the day: hold hands all the time – at breakfast and dinner, watching a film, going for a walk, or just doing nothing – until you die.

But, growing up, my mother told me some other things about boys. These changed over time – testament to her own transformation:

1. All boys want one thing only.

2. Sex has to go with love as its most pure expression – it should not happen for lust alone and certainly not before marriage.

3. Marriage is the ultimate goal – but first get engaged for at least a year.

4. In marriage, everything (not only bathing and talking) is shared 'as one': money, time, everything else.

5. But, merging is bad – you need to have your own ideas and be able to live alone, not lose yourself in a man.

6. On second thoughts, better than just being engaged, live with someone before getting married – for at least three years.

7. Sex before marriage is actually not that bad – as long as you're on the Pill.

8. It's OK to have a baby out of wedlock.

Being a mother

Joan

My mother Rose gave her life for her children. It rubbed off on me. More than anything, I wanted a baby.

From the day you were born, you made me laugh – your hair stood up on your head like Bugs Bunny – and I kissed the gynaecologist. But I also felt helpless and scared.

I wanted to give you culture – all the things I loved: books, music, art. So we could share it – unlike my mother and I. Culture from my mother? Apart from ballet, no way! She read historical novels, I read Anglo Saxon. I loved Beethoven, Brahms and Sibelius. She loved songs on the radio.

My mother loved to perform. I can still see her skipping into the dining room singing 'Let's all sing the Barmaid's Song'. That wasn't for me. I was bookish and serious. She didn't understand that. In fact she didn't understand me at all. Years after finishing my degree and already teaching English literature at university, she said to me one day: "You did Science didn't you?" I accepted her for what she was – funny, playful and loving. But, as much as there was love and the warmth of family, I often felt lonely.

When you arrived, most of all I wanted you to be happy and for us to be great friends.

Spooling back, the kitchen fades as I summon 'being great friends' – memory imprints:

'*Walking down Queensway past Whiteleys, it's foggy and chilly. I'm wearing my navy-blue duffel coat. Hers is the same, but woodland green. Hooking my arm through hers holds us close and makes me feel cosy. I can feel the heat of her breath wafting across my path through our chatter, warming my cheeks. I take a skip, to make my steps fall in with hers.*'

* * *

'*It's Sunday morning, I stand on a chair at the kitchen table, she stands on the floor, slightly behind me. We're both holding the wooden spoon to make a well in the flour.*'

* * *

'*On a hot, dry afternoon, in the red African earth we make deep holes for these roses – she does the digging, I pour the water, the sweat is standing out on our lips. We sit on our haunches, swigging iced tea from a jug, with lemon, plotting our war against aphids and snails, feeling pleased with ourselves.*'

* * *

'*Our hands work together, pulling the tail of yarn through the loop to cast on with thick wooden needles – good for knitting a jersey, but not for babies' booties – winding the wool round the back of the needle like this. "Now you have a go." "Sewing silk is trickier than cotton. Darts need to be perfectly sewn – not too tight or the bodice will pucker." "A tracing wheel can easily go off course – hold your hand around mine, feel the weight as you push." "This blue is perfect on you – it goes with your eyes."*'

* * *

'*Poems are easy to make – summon them forth and concoct wishes, lies and dreams – write them down, mush them up and read them out to each other.*'

* * *

'*Standing in front of a Rembrandt, she holds her hand up flat, to mask the right half of the portrait. Slowly sliding her hand to the left, she masks the other half – then back to the right, exposing the left half. "Can you see it, Cricket? The two halves aren't the same at all. That's because no human face is ever* symmetrical – one eye always looks more alive, the mouth is always different on either end – that's what great artists see.'"

* * *

'"Perfect pitch is a gift, so you have to learn music 'properly' – how to play piano, harmony, counterpoint, history of music – and also guitar. Then you can write your own music and sing your own songs." And I can – and I do – and I love it. So does she.'

* * *

'Sometimes, staying overnight en route to somewhere or another, I share her bed. On waking, she launches.

"You know, I've been thinking – economy of expression, that's what Yeats knew – and Shakespeare – I wonder if he…?"

"Hrmmhmmm." My eyes are barely open.

"My poetry group is driving me mad. I want to discuss – but all they want is to drink wine and read the poems out loud – nobody wants to analyse!!"

Scrunching into a fetal position, I squeeze my eyes shut, pretending I've gone back to sleep. I feel an exhausting mental monsoon coming my way and need to keep myself empty so I can take her in.

Her breakfast is always the same – a small bowl of muesli, plain yoghurt, a peach, neatly peeled and quartered, one slice of multigrain toast with marmalade, no butter. After, not during, a cup, sometimes two, of Earl Grey tea – weak, black, no sugar.

It's just as well I'm not hungry. There is almost nothing on the table that I eat. So I eat my guilt and ask her about the two Williams.'

* * *

'I'm standing outside, ringing the doorbell. As always, her smile is wide as she opens the door and her eyes spill delight at the sight of me. Stepping towards me she flowers her arms to welcome and wrap me.

"What have you been up to darling? Come see my new painting – there's a bud on my rose bush about to open – saw a wonderful film – well it wasn't Bergman, but still – and what are you reading darling?"

"Oh mom, someone you'd love – Elizabeth Strout – I'm learning so much from her about…"

"Oh, I must try her – I'm reading Elizabeth Taylor's short stories – you should try them – and how was your weekend?"

"It was lovely – we went to the Festival Hall…Mozart…"

"And I saw a marvellous concert – St. George's."

Shakespeare and Eliot, Yeats, Blake, Wordsworth, Chaucer, Dylan Thomas. Mozart, Marvel, Mahler, Bach, Beethoven, Rembrandt, Picasso, Moore, all the Impressionists, Ray, Kurosawa, Bergman, Lacan, Marx, Nureyev – a banquet of art, history, music, philosophy, politics, theatre, ballet, literature, film, course after course served up and fed without hold.

I always wanted to love her giving. And I did, and still do – who wouldn't! But sometimes her hungry heart made me feel like her lifeline – I'd wonder who she was feeding – me or her?'

Joan

When you were small you were easy – funny, curious, engaging, reasonable.

But when you grew older I found you hard to control. To be honest, I didn't want to control you at all – I wanted to give you ultimate freedom – but I had to – you became a rebellious schoolgirl.

I'm fifteen. My friends wear stockings and bikinis, go to mixed parties and dance with boys. But for me, it's white knee-socks, a 'nice, one-piece swimsuit' and endless fights about hems and hats, make-up and hot-pants.

I want to keep wanting to be her, girl-soldier in armour doing the splits, outrunning the boys. But peaches in a can! NO! It's the SIXTIES! For me, it's free love and the Pill, feeling groovy, not closing my eyes thinking of England and supper.

So I have to push back. Like Rosie, jumping the garden gate. Like my mother, kicking the tin, cutting her hair, giving up dancing.

Joan

Giving you independence was hard. I knew you'd leave me. Which was right. But the empty nest syndrome is real. Mothers don't want to let go. Daughters occupy space that no one else can fill. Ever. It's painful. What's lost? Maybe a piece of yourself.

I still believe in giving one's children ultimate freedom. To choose the person they want to live with. To live their lives the way they want to live. To do the work they love.

Before she married, my mother worked – dressing windows, making hats and costumes for the ballet. She loved it. When she married, she stopped. She said once, "I didn't marry your father to work for him."

I didn't want to be like my mother. I was determined to work – and do work I loved. And I did. For me, work was fulfillment. How lucky I was to be paid to do something I passionately wanted to do. That's what I wanted for you too – meaningful work, fulfilling and central to your life. I'm pleased with the way you've turned out, happy you embraced what I offered and ran with it, way past myself. It's mega-hard being a parent but if I could go back I'd do it exactly the same. Well maybe not quite – I'd be less strict about minis and make-up.

Joyce

On 24 September 1970, baby Joyce was born at our home in Johannesburg, delivered by my mother. Joyce's mother, Tiny, was sixteen – a year younger than me.

Tiny's mother was Lizzie, our African housekeeper, who lived with us. Lizzie was thrilled to be *gogo* (granny). But being a mother wasn't on *Tiny's* agenda.

Two days after the birth, my mother began to lactate. The new baby had taken its place in her empty nest.

In Apartheid South Africa, other than live-in domestic workers, 'non-white' people were strictly excluded from living in 'white areas'. Domestic workers living and working in white homes were not permitted to have their family members – partners and children – living with them. Those who were caught breaking the rules were arrested and sent away to the designated black (usually rural) area from which the family originally had come. Adoption of a black baby by a white family was illegal.

But my mother wanted to keep the baby. Lizzie's family, who lived in a poverty-stricken rural community three hours' drive from Johannesburg, were astonished. Whites didn't care about black babies. The love of this white woman could change this baby's life.

"Joyce can stay with you. All we need you to do is pay *lobola*" (the equivalent of a future bride price).

Hiding the fact that Joyce was living with us would carry a high risk. Random knocks on the door by the Special Branch of the SAP (South African Police) were common for anti-Apartheid families like ours.

Neighbours and their domestic workers could not be trusted to protect our secret. The penalty for discovery was jail.

Joan

One day Lizzie saw a police car draw up outside our house. Joyce was four. We hustled her into the laundry basket and passed her over the fence to the neighbour.

We couldn't live like that. It broke my heart to think of taking her away but I knew we'd have to leave South Africa.

Adoption

Seed pearls top this baby's feet
Above translucent soles
Magnets for joyous kisses
Dusty pink, this child of Africa

Where will her bright songs go,
Ululating throat-bursts
That tear the kopjies' silence?

Where will the dances go,
Foot-stomping rhythms
Gyrating around sangomas?

Where will her language go,
With its clicks that bring
The Kalahari scrub to life?

Fade it will,
Into the sibilant tongue
Of her adoptive home.

CARYN SOLOMON

All will be changed
This growing child, blanketed in love
Will suck transforming culture as her own.

Joan Solomon

Angry reformer

Joan
In actual fact, I had never accepted the status quo. In 1948, when the Nationalist government took over, formally instituting Apartheid, the university held anti-government meetings. I went to them all. That started to open my eyes and make me angry.

My cousin Baruch also opened my eyes. He wanted me to join ARM (African Resistance Movement). But I wouldn't join anything. Probably just as well. I'd have been arrested and thrown into jail with the rest of them.

After Baruch's arrest, I would drive every morning to pick up his wife, Yael, a doctor, to take her to work. Often I had a sense of being followed.

A policeman appeared one day, sitting in front of our house on his motorbike. When it began to rain, I went outside and invited him into the house. I left him in my study and went to the kitchen to make him some coffee. When I came back he was staring at an open book on my desk – I was working on Anglo Saxon poems.

"What is that?" he asked.
"Spy code," I told him.
His eyes moved to the oil painting on my wall – the naked black woman I painted.
"Who's that?"
"A friend of mine. And why are you asking these questions?"
He shook his head and drank his coffee. He didn't come again after that.

That was light-years away from the safety of here and now. Now we are laughing over our biscuits and tea at that dumb cop falling out of himself into a sea of dramatic thin and thick strokes and elaborate swirls on the serifs – Anglo Saxon script – *Beowulf*, sixth-century epic poem.

But both of us know that nothing was funny then, in that moment.

"That was brave of you mom – you were lucky he went away – you could have been dragged to jail."

91

Like the time I was dragged from the front row of the anti-Apartheid march to John Vorster Square Central Police Station, where, 'accidentally', Ahmed Timol and Matthews Mabelane – detained without trial – 'fell' to their deaths from the tenth floor, the same floor where Wellington Tshazibane and Neil Aggett were 'found' hanging from African scarves and blue jeans in their cells and Elmon Malele was made to stand for six hours being interrogated at night. He lost his balance, hit his head on the corner of a table and died of a brain haemorrhage. The subsequent inquest found he had died of 'natural causes'.

My chest tightens, filling with bile of memory rising. The sting of leather whips on my bare ankles. The sound of turnstiles clamping together like metal teeth. The raw barking and fetid odour of specially trained killer-Alsatians, more like wolves. The wet lips of flushed, boy-faced policemen watching me pee in an open toilet.

I wonder how many savage tales of gross, unspeakable acts have rolled into the cracks between these Georgian flagstones – I guess it can't have been many, here in civilised England. But then a sudden irony clenches my face, twists it into a shape that feels like tears – this house, my mother and father's home in Bristol, was built by people who made their fortunes buying and selling humans.

Grabbing my empty teacup, I fight back the urge to break my mother's flow – I know she knows what I'm thinking and feeling – it is she who has kept me alive to the fact that we all are somehow complicit in what people do and don't do to each other.

Joan

Why didn't I join ARM with my cousin Baruch?

Have I ever been known to join ANYTHING?

I wasn't an activist. My revolutionary friend, R, said I was 'just a reformer'. He meant it as an insult. I took it as a compliment. Being a reformer is much more useful – educate people to make choices and help themselves.

As an undergraduate, I made friends with Abe Mashugani, an artist. Ours being a 'white' university, Abe wasn't allowed to study there, only take a menial job as a 'demonstrator'.

During the holidays, under the auspices of the Institute of Race Relations, he and I used the university art studios to make wall charts to teach groups of black women basic reading skills. We took these on weekly trips to

Orlando Township, which later became Soweto, the police-run, segregated black township.

We used the charts as teaching aids to help non-literate people become proficient enough in reading and writing to form groups of their own and teach basic reading skills to others. This was the beginning of my life-long commitment to helping people speak with their own voice.

Then I looked for books that were easy enough to read without insulting the intelligence of adult women. There were none. My solution was to obtain books for their children – easy for mothers to read. But the only books for black children were rife with indoctrination – text and images showing black people exclusively as servants or in positions of subservience.

Some years later, I started running creative writing groups for teenagers in Soweto. The real aim was to create an opportunity for young people to talk about their lives – it was healing.

By now, Apartheid restrictions had become much more stringent. White doctors, police, church and government officials had special permission to enter Soweto. All other whites, and especially white teachers, were banned. Going there without a permit would land you in jail. I took one of Daddy's white coats, arrived there dressed as a doctor and ran my creative writing groups every Saturday for five years.

Soon I began to receive invitations to judge competitions at Soweto schools. I thought I might find children's books there, to use in my mothers' literacy groups. But most of these schools had no books at all, not even the ones showing black people as servants.

How do you learn to read with agency if you never see yourself reflected in books? I had to write them myself.

As no publisher would publish below cost to enable the people for whom they were intended to afford them, I set up my own imprint – Tswiri Books – and published five books myself. Now there were reading books for black children, which their parents could also read to them. The South African Bureau of Literacy used the Tswiri books all over the country with women's groups. Schools for black children soaked them up.

When Elaine Moss, well-known children's book critic, visited South Africa from London, wanting to see 'indigenous books published for children', the only books that existed were Tswiri books. She was astounded. "Hamish Hamilton has been looking for books like this for two years – culturally sensitive books for children in a very diverse society.

* * *

While still living in Johannesburg, I had been to the NAD (Native Affairs Department) to apply for a passport for Joyce, to take her to England to be educated. The white government official asked, "What's wrong with our education?"

I could have written a thesis on the schooling provided for black children during Apartheid. The application was refused.

At that time the NAD published a colour magazine which they sent to Europe to show what wonderful things whites in SA were doing for blacks! One day, to my surprise, I saw in one of these magazines a two-page, colour spread about Tswiri books, featuring Joyce! I was furious – no permission was ever asked and none given. But, back I went to the damned NAD to apply for a passport to take Joyce to Europe to promote Tswiri books. The man at the NAD had the gall to ask me to look at some of the children's stories he'd written!

But we got the passport and that is how I managed to take Joyce out of South Africa.

* * *

After we'd settled in London, I wrote and photo-illustrated a collection of 'culturally sensitive children's books for a diverse society'. Hamish Hamilton published them. One was even selected as a 'Best Children's Book of the Year'.

Today they're still in schools and children's libraries all over Britain. I don't know if they've made a difference.

Nearly forty years on, turning the pages of *Everybody's Hair*, *Gifts and Almonds*, *Joyce's Day* and all the others, Michel Foucault's words spring to mind:

"People know what they do; frequently they know why they do what they do; but what they don't know is what 'what they do' does." (Madness and Civilization: A History of Insanity in the Age of Reason, 1961).

Mom, you did what you did, you did your best and you'll never know what you did has done, or how many children have opened those books. But know that those who have, have walked through doors opened by you, have found themselves reframed by simple, human stories born of your steadfast passion for planting seeds and your deepest sense of what truly matters. And that will have made them feel that they matter too.

Becoming 'me'

Joan

I started off being like my mother. In her era, women weren't supposed to have needs or make demands. As a young woman, she fought her father, suffered his insults when she 'went out to work'. But he won — when she married, she took her place in the home and lived out her own silent history. I thought that's how women had to behave.

One day, after some years lecturing, I discovered that white males at the university earned more than I did with the same training and much more experience than many of them had! Black men earned even less than I did. And if you were a black woman you stayed home and did the washing because it wasn't worth leaving the house. From then on, I was not South African, English, Jewish or anything else. I defined myself only as 'woman.' You could say that was the day I became a feminist.

I marched into the faculty office and demanded to know why I was paid less than the white men.

But no one heard me. Nothing changed. I carried on being the person I'd always been, suppressing my voice and my needs.

Oh, I know that courage and blast of hers, devoid of guile and politics, just like a child. Sadly, for those in the inner sanctum of White Male Power, she was little more than a high-pitched noise, shouting to know why her chocolate biscuit was smaller.

Joan

Once, at a medical dinner, a world-renowned doctor sitting beside me put his hand on my thigh. Later that night, I said to Daddy, "If ever I'm seated next to that man again I'm going to say something."

Believe it or not, at the next dinner there he was, seated beside me again. Again, he touched my thigh. I bent down under the table and loudly said, "I think there's a dog down here, who put his paw on my thigh." I made a big show of looking under the table some more, stood up and said, even louder, "No dog under here. It must be you!"

Women should speak, not blame. It's up to us to protect ourselves.
I didn't formally join the 'cause' or burn my bra. I simply defined myself as a feminist.

* * *

Daddy was dedicated to his work. Our whole life was a series of interruptions by people NEEDING him. Several times a night I'd put his dinner back in the oven. In that job, it's all or nothing. In his case it was ALL, right from the early days of our marriage. And he was very, very giving. So many times, at four in the morning he'd be called out. Being a doctor's wife you always come second to those interruptions.

For a split second, my stomach churns and then I'm sitting with Mom, Dad and Ryan at dinner – the only meal our family had together each day. Those were warm, together times, chatting about the day, telling stories, asking questions, exchanging ideas, Dad building crazy towers with random objects on the table. But those times seemed also to be the phone's cue to ring, the cue for my mother's jaw to tighten, her eyes to go dead. Even now when the phone rings during a meal, I lose the will to eat.

Joan
In the beginning, I tried to be playful. Then I thought of running groups for doctors' wives. Over the years, it builds resentment and anger.

From my bedroom her voice is little more than a gentle breathing out. It's midnight, time for her nightly tryst. Straining to hear, sometimes I catch the odd phrase.

"Pilgrim soul…yes, pilgrims do wander, but that's not it …he's talking of utter devotion…"

"…Maude Gonne's continual rejection…tragic…inspired him to greater heights…and love is also darkness…sometimes"

I don't understand, but, lying still in the dark, I sense it – my mother dissolving into the conversation, like being in a warm lake where skin and water are one.

I slide out of bed, silently creep barefoot to the door, peep into the hallway. There she is in her flimsy, lime-green, baggy t-shirt, dishevelled locks flung to one side, phone to her ear, looking for all the world like one of her tousled students, her beloved *W. B. Yeats – Collected Poems* cradled in her lap.

Faintly, through the phone, a man's voice.

"…loved your beauty…" "…loved the sorrows…"

Tonguing their way to each other through each line of 'When We Are Old'. Her cheeks glow with the taste of it.

Daddy is fast asleep. Tomorrow he'll replace the left hip of a woman, seventy-two years old. Three hours on his feet to give her fifteen years more on hers. Her gratitude will know no bounds.

I'm only twelve, but my heart breaks – for my unsuspecting father – and for my mother, waiting, waiting in the wings – waiting for her turn to star in her husband's show. And while she waits, winding her way into the light of her best friend, R.

But that will run its course. Overdosed on poems and picnics and play, defeated by Daddy's inviolable place in her heart, R will leave her sprawled in a ditch of dashed expectations, alone in her soul's dark night.

Joan

Daddy never stopped me from doing what I wanted to do. It was me who had stopped me. I know now that my fight wasn't with him. I was fighting myself, trying to free myself from what my mother had been and what she had taught me to be. And I wanted to make sure that the way I was didn't affect you. Separating from daddy allowed me to grow and come back to the marriage in a way that gave me the joy I ended up having.

When I came back, he said I had grown selfish. He was right, I had – living alone for nine years changed me completely – for the better. I made my needs known.

Finding out he'd been involved with someone else during the time we were apart, I felt betrayed and angry. Even though I was the one who left. His gift to me – he understood. I still can't believe he forgave me.

He never gave up loving her, no matter what she did.

Joan

It took me thirty years to say sorry. Just before he died, I said:

"I'm sorry for all the shit I caused you. I had to forgive myself before I could ask your forgiveness."

And you know what he did? He put out his hand and squeezed mine. It still makes me cry.

Thirty more years — a second chance, a reprieve — to re-create 'the space between', to find a way to take his love without losing herself. Thirty years to grow together, until she could hardly tell herself apart from him — but this time it would be her choice.

* * *

Joan and Louis set up home in a beautiful Georgian house and found a new school for Joyce in Bristol, where my father took up the Chair of Orthopaedic Surgery at Bristol University. But leaving the small, two-bedroomed cottage in Willesden Lane which Joan and Joyce had shared for nine years was no clean break. For two years, Joan took the train to London and stayed in the cottage for three days a week, attending her course in book design, visiting galleries, seeing friends, holding on to who she'd become. The rest of the time she spent planting herself in Bristol, alongside Louis.

* * *

Today, casting my gaze through the broad kitchen window, beyond the wide window-ledge with its line-up of coloured glass and brightly-glazed bowls parading their show of fresh-picked blooms and ripe tomatoes, I find myself in a painting — my mother's garden — a quintessential, English fairy-tale autumn scene (filtered through African eyes). Ruddy clusters and spreads fading to gold, last-season crackling yellows and greens, purple leaves beginning to circle down, a grey squirrel crouched in a slant of light, branches stretching to winter.

A family of well-fed foxes lives in the small wooden shed covered in creeping roses, some still in bloom, behind the row of espaliered apples, and down at the garden's end, tucked in a blousy abundance of lace-cap hydrangeas, the tiny Victorian Wendy-house — original Victorian lead-pane windows still uncracked — filled with relics of play: miniature chairs, cups, saucers, teapots, dinners of dried petals and dead woodlice.

This is a place of enchantment – it looks like it's planted itself. But this is the garden they *made*, together – Joan, designing, digging, planting and pruning, Louis mounting and tending the Spanish wall pots. Overflowing with colour each spring, inspired by road trips and lazy family summers in Spain.

An eerie tinkle trickles into the kitchen from somewhere inside the plum tree – my mother's birthday chimes, brought by Dad from the old Johannesburg house – reminds us it's breezy out there.

"The garden's looking so lovely, Mom."

"Yes, but it all needs pruning – I wish I could get my hands round my secateurs – these fingers don't work anymore."

2020

My mother has been clearing her study.

"Darling, I've kept some things for you. Maybe you can use them in your story."

She hands me a flat, rectangular, bright orange cardboard box, the kind used for photographic paper. On the lid is written AGFA PROFESSIONAL.

In her sixties, Joan enrolled for an MA in Film and Photography. Inside the box is her final project – a parody of a family album, entitled 'The Family Snaps'.

There's a hand-written letter to her mother and nine images.

Joan's mother appears in five of the images, her father in three. Both young parents are played by actors.

Two of the images show pictures on the walls – Joan at three and her and Louis' wedding photo.

The final image is Joan, a self-portrait.

The piece went on exhibition at Bristol's Watershed, accompanied by a short blurb, in which my mother refers to her own mother, Rose, as follows:

'Conspirators in our own exiles we were, I for survival, she for catching in me the lost echoes of her own childhood and remnants of her dreams. Here my silence began, the silence of the good daughter, pleasing and achieving, fulfilling my mother's unfulfilled longings, but taking me, most painfully for both of us, outside her understanding and away from her and myself.'

shocked to see how little space you had in the Old People's Home, but I know it is what you need; to move safely from bed, to basin, to chair. How hard you tried, my Mother, to reach into the world – but who was there to listen to you? (For that matter, who heard the voice of my working class father?) To find a place for yourself you had to be a "good wife" and a "good mother" and once in your accorded place, you disappeared. In your children you strove to articulate your life – an ideal self. It has cost us our own emotional history, just as being what was expected of you, has cost you yours. We are all of us, always in the imaginary, trying and failing to reach an ideal self. Neatness and badges for deportment your mother wanted of you and you in your turn elicited this from me. My being your model child gratified you and you gave me much in return, but at what cost. There was no space for my wrestling emotional self. I learnt to bury it.

　　How good a mother you have been hasn't in the end anything to do with excellence. Ironically, it is your own exemplary strength which has helped me to struggle towards the dishevelled, "dark" feelings you so didn't want to acknowledge. Now paradoxically, in the very shaping of a critique of performance, I am still caught up in the crisis of performing. Such is the nature of representation. I take this risk to share my understanding. I know you wont hear all this, but in loving you, it needs to be said.

　　　　　　　　　　　　Your child

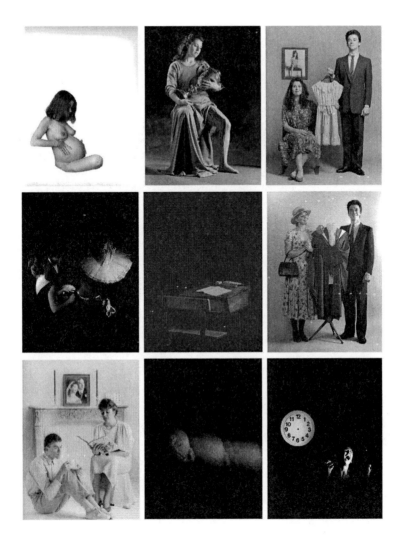

That word, 'outside'. From her very beginning, my mother ached – like someone abandoned – an orphan perhaps – longing for something, afraid of being 'not here'.

No matter what changed, or how she fought, it seemed to me that one thing stayed the same: she always longed for the nirvana of a partner with whom she could leap into an infinity of shared passion – entwined in a mutual high, seeing the world through one pair of eyes, in constant embrace and perfect step, their selves reflected in each other.

Sometimes I wonder what I would have done in her shoes – but then, I wouldn't have been in her shoes, precisely because *she* was, stepping forward with fire, burning that path, creating a way for me – to take my place, to make my sound, to keep my silence, to choose who to be, to walk as myself.

I have never wanted to merge, to melt myself into an all-encompassing, all-consuming 'oneness', to be someone's 'other half'. I like my own space, I breathe my own breath, easily being me. This has been my mother's gift, won for me through a lifetime of forging her way to be her.

* * *

A few months later, my mother and I are talking about my 'story':

"I'm glad you can use that old project of mine, darling. There are also more photos of family, and some of my poems – there were more, but I threw them away."

"Oh no! Why? Why did you do that? Please keep whatever you've written – it's treasure for me."

"They were all unfinished."

"Mom! What is 'finished'? This conversation, right now, would we ever throw it away because it's unfinished? No!"

"That's true – we wouldn't."

CROSSING BOUNDARIES, LOOKING FORWARD

Veena Siddharth

India and America

Introduction

Saroja Arunachalam Siddharth was born in 1935 in the British Empire, came of age in newly independent India and left for the U.S. when she was 23. She has been an American citizen for longer than she ever lived in India. A widow now, she lives in a retirement community on the Main Line, a green and prosperous suburb of Philadelphia.

"Why did you come here?" It is a frequent question, and a reminder that she is still an outsider in a country she first arrived in more than 60 years ago.

Her training as a paediatrician changed life's possibilities. It gave her the option to leave India, the freedom to choose her husband, an intellectually fulfilling career and the power to help people. It also played to her strengths. As a 24-year-old resident at Bellevue Hospital in New York she could identify the symptoms of a rare tropical illness based on a lecture she had heard in medical school five years before. When confronted with a child screaming in pain, she could stay centered and comfort the parents with a detailed explanation of the treatment. Intense displays of emotion were what she saw in others, but not herself. She would stay calm, comforted by science.

She found her identity and authority in medicine and was the doctor trusted and sought out by migrant workers in India and single mothers in the US. She and my father could not imagine another profession as relevant or practical, and were aghast to see me, the first in the family to have the luxury of an American education, choose human rights over medicine. Now I understand that our professions are not as different as it had seemed when I strayed. My mother has influenced me in ways I am only now understanding.

We have our tensions – I am expressive, emotional, and reactive while she does not easily display her vulnerability. If pushed, she will talk about the past but the voids of the stories she doesn't tell are tangible. During the pandemic, my visits to see her from Costa Rica were replaced with phone conversations. I asked her questions I never thought to broach before – were you scared to get on that plane to the US? Was it strange to be asked out on a date in New York? Who was your first American friend? How many children did you want?. If I go too far she shuts down the conversation. The process demands persistence.

Being American

October 2020, Costa Rica and Haverford, Pennsylvania

"*Paati,* that doesn't sound safe!"

My 12-year-old son, Kailash, sounds alarmed. He is talking to his grand-mother on WhatsApp, a daily routine during the pandemic. The wait until he finishes the call is excruciating. When he is done, he rushes over to me.

"She wants to go in person to deliver her ballot. Mom, even if she wears a mask, that's dangerous! Can you talk to her?"

I picture my mother's prickly reaction if I were to question her plans. She has an adolescent's opposition when told what to do. Yet voting is a serious matter. Saroja hasn't missed voting in an election since she got her U.S. citizenship, when she first cast her ballot for Jimmy Carter in 1976. But even before becoming American she followed U.S. politics. Kennedy, Hubert Humphrey and McGovern. She and my father always favored Democratic candidates. The vote in 2020 seems more urgent than ever and with the danger of Democratic votes not being counted, she is deter-mined to thinking of her grandchildren's future propels her to ignore the dangers of the pandemic.

In the end my sister convinces her to mail in her ballot. On their next call, Kailash thanks her for moving Pennsylvania to the Democrats.

A Return

Coimbatore, December 2019

I hold my mother's hand as we slowly descend the stairs of the plane to Coimbatore airport. She lifts her sari so as not to trip. She insists "I can do it myself" and pushes me aside but I don't let go. We look up at the blue-green *Nilgiri* Mountains, shimmering in the distance. The elevation at these foothills makes the air refreshingly crisp.

We met two days before in Chennai after long flights – my mother Saroja travelling from Philadelphia and I from Costa Rica. We are unaware of our good fortune. Had we waited just a few months later, COVID-19 would have made such a trip unimaginable.

As we load our luggage into a taxi, I look at my mother leaning on her walking stick and imagine her 60 years ago, getting ready to leave India. Her major life transitions happened away from India, meeting my father and getting married, qualifying as a paediatrician, having two children. Now at 84, she is returning to Coimbatore to see her sisters Padmini and Meenakshi. She needs assistance for the journey, and I have happily complied, bringing my husband and two children along.

My father enjoyed talking about the past, but my mother has the immigrant's preference to look ahead. As a child, when I asked her questions about growing up in India, I rarely got much beyond hagiography – paens to my grandfather's liberal beliefs or the value of studying. Her memories lacked the detail, texture and humour of what I heard from family members in India. My aunts would tell me how she pretended to be drunk after her older brother administered cod liver oil, how she swiped her cousin's bicycle when he came to visit from the office, how she would spend hours in the corner with a book ignoring everyone in the room, how she sang along in English to Christmas carols while sitting next to the radio. Her mother's illness left a gap that was partially filled by loving relatives, a kind cook and a father who believed in her. But it also meant all the children had to become self-reliant at a young age.

When Saroja first moved to Coimbatore in 1945 the movement for independence from Britain was in full throttle. As a girl, she sang "God Save the King" every morning in school while the tumult of opposition to British rule seethed around her. During her girlhood and adolescence, World War II ended and a few years later India became a new nation. There were sweeping shifts in the expectations of women. Saroja's mother Bhavani left school to get married and had her first child at 16. Two decades later, Saroja became a doctor and went on to choose her own husband at 26, marrying in the U.S. But the expectations associated with being a good wife never went away and were simply added onto the newer expectations to have a successful career.

Little of this past is evident from the taxi. Pedestrians are wrapped in shawls against the winter chill, which is like a spring day in London. A prosperous class of Indians shop for organic vegetables, ayurvedic shampoos, designer clothes and fancy luggage. Young men and women walk holding hands. There are Christmas decorations on some of the storefronts. I don't see the poverty that I saw in India as a child.

It suddenly seems plausible to imagine having grown up in India. Of course, this makes no sense, as my mother met my father in New York, and I was born in Massachusetts. Still, the sensation of wanting to be part of a place and belonging here gnaws at me. We moved to India for two and a half years when I was six years old. I was a Canadian child and felt like a foreigner, needing extra tuition to catch up in Hindi. Indian schools were more intense and competitive, so much so that when we moved to the

U.S. I was put two years ahead. But what if I had been born and brought up in India? What would it feel like not to be an outsider?

"Mom, do you ever wonder what your life would have been like if you hadn't left?" I ask her idly. It is a speculative question, a daydream.

I am jolted by her anger.

"I did nothing wrong. I never think about that," She retorts.

I wonder why she is so quick to take offence. She turns away and I feel the stormy silence. It dawns on me that she feels reprimanded for having left.

"No, that's not what I meant," I start. "I just wanted to know whether you ever wonder…"

But she is still talking, and I understand in a way I hadn't before

"I wouldn't have ever been able to be successful here. I had no connections; my family couldn't help me. Things were getting difficult for Brahmins and getting a job was becoming very hard. I…"

She trails off. I feel my shoulders tense. I have done it again – gone too far in asking a question and she has taken offence. I wanted an emotional conversation about how she felt to be back but that is not her.

Celebration on the rooftop

Coimbatore, September 1945

Saroja woke up to cheering and singing in the streets. Her family had moved to Coimbatore five months earlier from the small city of Devakottai and this big city was overwhelming, with so many people. Her older sister Padmini, who was 11, rolled up their sleeping mat. She pulled Padmini's arm, and they ran outside to see where the noise was coming from but there houses blocked the way. They opened the almirah to get their school uniforms and put on their long skirts and blouses.

On the veranda, Arunachalam, "*Appa*" (father in Tamil), was listening closely to the news. His face was beaming. When he saw them, he said with a laugh "The Japanese have surrendered!" Saroja saw the relief in his face. He had been worried when the Japanese bombed Madras.

She ran to the kitchen to tell their cook Hariharan the news. "The war is over!" she cried out. She glanced at her mother Bhavani, sitting on the floor cross-legged and chopping vegetables. Bhavani didn't register what the commotion was about, nor did she realize that Saroja's tenth birthday was in a few weeks. She was muttering to herself, but Saroja couldn't make out what she was saying. She hardly remembered what her mother had been like before she had fallen ill. Soon after the birth of Saroja's youngest sister Meenakshi when Saroja was five years old, Bhavani suffered a breakdown. She was not able to fully function as a mother again. She sometimes heard voices, spoke to herself and occasionally did not know where she was. She paced up and down the veranda of their house and washed her hands often. Padmini, who was two years older, remembered when Bhavani was engaged with her children. She described a gentle and kind woman with an artistic eye who enjoyed indulgences such as Huntley Palmer English biscuits and Christmas cake.

Appa needed help to run a household of seven young children while he travelled around Tamil Nadu for work as a company lawyer. He found Hariharan after Bhavani had her breakdown. Hariharan was much more than a cook. Along with caring for his own family, he kept track of what treats each child especially liked. Despite wartime rations, a tight budget and no refrigeration or electrical appliances, he managed to produce *vadais, bondas* and other special treats. It was Hariharan who remembered all the children's birthdays with a sweet. Saroja eagerly looked forward to what he would make for her – perhaps a rice pudding, *payasam*, or peanut candy with jaggery, a molasses type sugar.

Hariharan had his quirks. After school when Saroja would go into the kitchen to see what was for tiffin, she would sometimes see him scolding a pot, pan or ladle for slipping from his hands. Bhavani was always nearby, but she drifted in and out of her own world. Instinctively, Hariharan knew that Bhavani would thrive if she was occupied in contributing to the household with him and he was a kind presence with her in the kitchen, finding ways she could help when she was able.

This morning Saroja wasn't sure what Japanese surrender meant. She knew Indians were fighting under the British in Japan and Malaya, and she had seen protests against the British recruiting Indians for the war. Appa supported Gandhiji, who had been put in prison several times for opposing the British.

Saroja's 7-year-old sister Uma asked Appa the question on all of their minds. Was it a holiday? Could they skip school? Appa smiled and said no, it was a normal school day. With that tantalizing possibility gone, Saroja and Padmini went back to packing their bags and went outside to be picked up. In Devakottai they would have walked to school with Appa, but Coimbatore was too big. Now Krishnan, who helped Appa in his law office, took them in a horse cart to the Government Girls School.

Krishnan arrived thirty minutes late and told Appa there were crowds of people on the street outside. He said,

"Saar, I think it will take some time for me to reach the office today."

Appa shook his head from side to side to convey that was fine,

"I don't think any of us will be working today Krishnan!"

The girls climbed into the cart and gazed open-mouthed at the cars, buses, cyclists, and people gathered in the streets, some to celebrate and a few to protest. They saw a special bus full of white people waving British flags, the men with red, sunburned faces and the women with large hats. The protestors tried to go toward the bus, but the police pushed them back. Saroja remembered that Appa had told them that the British evacuated their citizens from as far as Malta and Malaysia to Coimbatore due to the war.

Today Krishnan didn't pick up any other girls and headed straight to school. People on the streets cheered and waved banners that said "Victory" and "Long Live the King". The sweet scent of jasmine floated by the girls when they passed the corner where women strung flowers together. Men stood outside the coffee stalls to pour strong, milky coffee from one steel tumbler to the other. Just before the turnoff for school they saw police standing in front of a group of men who held up a banner that said, "Quit India."

Saroja remembered the *Quit India* signs from Devakottai. One morning in 1942 when she was seven, the "Quit India" movement burned down the Devakottai High Court during the night, blocking the road to her school. Padmini and Saroja couldn't attend school until the court was repaired. The girls were thrilled to miss school but didn't understand what "Quit India" meant. Appa explained that it was a movement for Indian independence. The leaders of the independence movement were angry that Indian soldiers had fought for Britain in World War I without being rewarded with independence. The girls knew that Appa supported the independence movement, but he did not say much about it. Not everyone did.

When St. Mary's Convent reopened, Appa dropped the girls off before rushing to the Court to argue his cases, mostly in company law. The smell of charred wood lingered and the sisters saw the blackened walls of the Court visible in the distance, along with police guards and checkpoints. Soon Appa stopped wearing the English style clothes of a barrister at the court and switched to khadi, the hand-spun cotton that Gandhi encouraged people to wear to support Indian-made goods. It was becoming more accepted to openly support independence and Appa talked to the children about the freedom fighters and what they wanted for a new India.

Now, as the horsecar wove through the crowds, Saroja watched Padmini precisely fold her homework and put it in her bag. Her sister's meticulous ritual made Saroja realize with dismay that yet again, she had forgotten to bring her hastily scrawled Maths homework. The teachers would surely punish her.

Saroja hated Maths and resented Padmini for not only excelling at it, but also being tidy and organized – qualities that eluded her. On most afternoons when they reached home from school, Padmini hung her bag carefully on the hook on the back of the door, changed out of her uniform and folded it. In contrast, Saroja leapt out of the horse cart and hurled her bag to the floor. She raced outside to grab her brother's bicycle and pedaled furiously to her favourite tree. When she got there, she would throw the bicycle to one side and climb up to perch on a branch with the latest issue of "*Kalki*" a Tamil weekly that had stories and puzzles for children.

From the back of the horse cart, Saroja turned to the commotion around them and excitedly pointed to the "Quit India" protestors wearing simple white cloth wrapped around them.

"*Paare!* Look!" she cried out

There were men and women wearing khadi *lungis* and saris walking with signs that said, "Quit India, Do or Die". The British had arrested the protestors in Devakottai and might do so here as well. It was dangerous. They couldn't linger to see what would happen.

Krishnan stopped the cart and the girls jumped out. The Government Girls School of Coimbatore was far bigger than St Mary's Convent in Devakottai with many girls they still didn't know. In Devakottai there had been Christian prayers led by the French nuns every day but now there were no prayers. Instead, there were Anglo Indian teachers with exotic names like "Mrs. Connor" and "Miss O'Brien". These teachers seemed more Indian and more accessible than the French nuns, despite their English names. Saroja wondered what they thought of the celebrations of Britain's victory in the war. Were their loyalties with the Indians or the English?

Today in Maths, as she had feared, Miss Michaels called Saroja to explain where her homework was. She stood up next to her chair. "I left it at home Miss" she murmured faintly. Miss Michaels said sternly that she had to do extra homework tonight and would be called up in front of everyone again if she didn't bring her homework in tomorrow. After Maths she had English and Tamil. At lunch she opened her tiffin box to have yogurt and rice packed by Hariharan and then there was a break with games and music. On the way home Saroja liked to make Krishnan laugh by whistling the English songs they sang in music class. The day ended with sewing class. "Lalitha Teacher" asked to inspect their stitching. During the war only the coarsest cotton was available and when Saroja handed in her hemming Lalitha Teacher said "*What kind of cloth is this! If you blow your nose on it, you will get scratched!*" How could her teacher didn't know that this rough burlap was the only cloth available during the war?

Today it was hard to concentrate at school. There was so much noise and commotion outside. The teachers were distracted, looking at the clock with their minds elsewhere.

When the school day ended, the girls raced to the rooftop to play with their friends while they waited for Krishnan. They were slight and wiry in their long blue skirts and white blouses. Each girl had tight plaits, smooth, and glistening with coconut oil. They ran after each other, laughing and finally free from the discipline of their schoolteachers. As they played hopscotch and skipped rope, they sensed that the rhythm of the city was different. There were even more crowds than there had been in the morning.

Dusk fell suddenly. They had never been at school when it was dark. At first, they weren't bothered. They could play for longer than usual. As it became darker and they heard the shouting from the streets they felt a frisson of danger and looked out onto the city, wondering what had happened. The streets were still crowded. Some were cheering in jubilation that the Japanese had surrendered, and the war was over, but there were a few protestors carrying Quit India signs. Who should they be cheering? The British? Or Gandhi and the other freedom fighters in jail?

A girl named Alice Epen waited quietly for her mother. She was a Christian from Kerala whose mother was a lawyer and drove her to school in a company car. Saroja said to Padmini "Her mother is doing a job for fathers!" After Alice left, the girls were alone on the roof of the school. What would they do? Had Krishnan forgotten them? They watched the traffic flow until finally, they heard the school guard calling. Krishnan had arrived. He looked shaken and worried, explaining "I could not get through the crowds"

For a long time what stood out about this day for Saroja was the thrill of being left at school. Only many years later did she absorb that the war's end foreshadowed the British leaving India.

An Accidental Doctor

When she became a doctor Saroja entered a world of opportunities and freedoms apart from her siblings. Yet she was not the first one in the family to aspire to enter medical school. Her older sister Radha had always been an excellent student and after high school Radha took the entrance exams for the most selective medical school in South India, the Christian Medical School (CMC) at Vellore. There was only one seat every year for a non-Christian and Radha's exam results were stellar, earning her that coveted spot. At the end of her first year, she was the highest-ranking student in her class.

During her second year of medical school, a marriage proposal came for Radha from a well-known and prosperous family. Appa's brothers told him it was Radha's duty to take it. If she refused, it could block prospects of finding grooms for the younger girls, as marriages needed to occur in age order. And Bhavani's illness could make finding grooms doubly difficult.

Saroja, Chennai, 1954

Arunachalam felt his duty to his other children and persuaded Radha to drop out. It was not an easy decision and one he wrestled with for a long time afterwards. Not only was Radha's academic performance exemplary, but after Bhavani's illness she had taken on tremendous responsibilities to support the family in her kind and gentle manner. After she left CMC, a prominent doctor teaching there wrote her a chiding letter, saying she had wasted a valuable place, taking it from someone who would finish. She spent the next decade exploring options for continuing her medical studies while raising her family, but it proved impossible.

Saroja was four years younger, bright and curious, but only did well in what she liked. However, when she was fifteen, she became fascinated with chemistry and biology. Seeing Radha go to medical school made the idea of becoming a doctor tangible and suddenly she wanted it more than anything. She studied with her friend Pichammal for the medical exam. On the day the results came out, her father's oldest brother came to visit and proclaimed "Saroja has done very well!" He had seen the postings for admission to medical school and Saroja's name was on it, helped by her excellent results in chemistry. Sadly, Pichammal didn't make it that year.

Saroja was taken aback, as was the family. No one had expected her to have such high marks. Her perception of herself shifted and she began to think "I can do this!" She spent the next five years taking the long bus ride to Madras Medical School, befriending classmates on the bus but staying apart from the hostel students who seemed to inhabit a more elite world. She graduated in 1958 at the age of 22, completing what her older sister Radha had started. Some of her female classmates got married but she made it clear to Appa that she wanted to finish her studies and training before getting married.

After graduation, Saroja worked at a hospital in Madras. Many of her classmates left for the UK, and some even ventured to the US, but she had no such plans. Except for her older brother Rajan, who had spent a year in Manchester to study textile production, she didn't know anyone who had been to the West. Leaving India never occurred to her.

She often took breaks on her way back from the hospital to go to the United States Information Service (USIS) library in Madras. One day she walked into the reading room and recognized Shamsuddin, a classmate from medical school. He was at a desk, intently filling out a form. She stopped to say hello. He told her he was filling out an application to an American program that accepted recent medical graduates to work as doctors in the U.S. While U.S. immigration rules almost totally banned non-European immigrants, there was a shortage of doctors and under this scheme, Indians could live in the US for five years, although working in less desired inner-city hospitals with low salaries.

Shamsuddin had an extra application. "Here, take it," he said, handing it to her with a nod. "You don't have to pay the fee as I already paid for the two forms." Her mind started racing. America? She thought of the pictures in *Life* magazine of gleaming cities and mountains. Like Shamsuddin, she had no connections to find a job in a good hospital in Madras or family money to establish her own practice. Her future in India seemed uncertain. The prospect of going to America was scary yet exciting. Would Appa say yes?

On the bus ride back home, she imagined herself in a modern city with skyscrapers and cars as big as boats. It would be an escape from all the expectations and tiresome questions about her future from her uncles and her father's friends. She could ask her friend Geeta to apply also. Geeta was from a progressive family in Karnataka and lived in the hostel. Like Saroja, she had been allowed to stay unmarried during her medical studies.

When she got home, she broached the subject carefully while Appa was reading the newspaper and having his tea.

"There is a chance to get a job in America as a doctor. I can train and they will pay for a five-year stay. All I need is the money for the ticket."

She paused and waited, wondering what he would say. He looked up from the newspaper and said.

"Why not? It could be a good opportunity for you."

She sighed with relief that Appa seemed happy to decide for himself and not consult with his brothers.

"When you return you can find a job easily here," he said, getting up to return to the office. She went out to the veranda and filled out the form before he could change his mind.

She had no idea where in the US she would go if she was accepted. She posted the envelope and returned to her daily life of going to the hospital and coming home on the bus. It faded from her mind.

Two months later, she came home to find an envelope waiting for her from the American Consulate. To her surprise, she had been offered a position at a Catholic hospital in Brooklyn. Now it was real! At the hospital the next day Geeta ran to her and grabbed her arm. "I got St Louis!" All Saroja could think of was the film *Meet Me in St. Louis* with Judy Garland. She looked on a map and was sad to see that it was at least a two-day bus journey from New York. Geeta said they had a classmate who just graduated in the class below who was also going to New York. His name was Siddharth, and he was organizing a get-together for those going to the US. Geeta knew him and would ask if they could attend.

The next day Geeta told Saroja that Siddharth wanted them to come to a lunch for a small group of classmates who would be going to America. To Saroja, they were a more privileged group who kept apart from the other students. She was glad that there would be at least two that she knew: Shamsuddin who had given her the application and Srinivasan, who was from a poor family but known for his stellar grades.

The two young women made their way the following week to a stately home on Mount Road in central Madras, wearing their best saris. Outside was a large placard with the name of the house, "*Chandrika*" At the gate a watchman showed them in. A driver was sitting outside next to a white Ambassador.

Siddharth came outside to greet them with the familiarity of an old friend. He saw them looking at the house's name and said "Chandrika was my father's sister who died at 14. She was very good at her studies and impressed all the Britishers he worked with. He misses her every day."

Saroja realized she had seen Siddharth many times during medical school, but they had never spoken. He was the president of the student body and had the easy confidence that comes with being well-spoken and from a prominent family. He would come to classes in the morning on his motorcycle with friends who also took such luxuries for granted. He lived in a different world of status and privilege. He was popular and outgoing, known for his scathing and hilarious impressions of their medical school professors.

Siddharth peered at them through round-framed glasses. He had a square jaw and friendly eyes. "You must be hungry! Come, come" he said, smiling warmly and gesturing for them to enter the house. "My mother has made North Indian food, *parathas* and *korma*. Have you both gotten your assignments in the U.S?" he asked

Geeta said, "I'm going to St Louis and Saroja is going to New York."

Siddharth clapped his hands and turned to Saroja. "I'm going to be in New York as well! I'm leaving in a month."

Saroja was taken aback. She hardly knew Siddharth and had expected him to be stand-offish, not this warm and exuberant person.

They took off their sandals and entered the house. Siddharth's father came towards them, walking with a cane and a limp from what appeared to be a stroke. He had his son's strong features but was shorter, quieter and more serious. He congratulated them on their opportunity to go to America, telling them he had studied in England at Cambridge in the 1930s, later taking the difficult exam for the British administration, the "Indian Civil Service". He had been one of the few Indians allowed to enter this elite cadre and was posted to North India, given a senior position in the administration of India's most populous state, Uttar Pradesh. Saroja realized that as a Tamilian he had had to acquire fluency in Hindi and Urdu, as foreign to her as Greek, and socialize with the British officers, a complex feat of cultural and linguistic adaptability.

Siddharth's mother Kalpakam welcomed them, a handsome woman with a confident, dignified bearing. While their cook brought out samosas and a mint chutney, Kalpakam described her trips to England and Europe, when Siddharth's father was getting his barrister qualification in London. She was a strict vegetarian and warned them: "Foreigners don't understand what we mean by vegetarian! In France they brought the meat stew to me and pulled the meat out!" Saroja wasn't sure she would stay a vegetarian but dared not say it.

Siddharth (middle with glasses) with his brothers and parents, Chennai 1955

Kalpakam talked about her father, a prominent lawyer and philanthropist in Madras whose name, Subbaraya Aiyar, Saroja recognized. He had founded a university, a school and a foundation to do charity work. Kalpakam's great aunt had founded Kalakshetra, a globally known music and dance academy. She asked Saroja and Geeta who their parents were and what they did. While they came from educated backgrounds, it was clear that neither of their families occupied the same social sphere. Saroja could see Kalpakam making the complicated and necessary appraisal of their relative social levels. Later, Saroja told her sisters that going to Siddharth's house was like entering a different world, one she would never see if not for the shared plan to go to America.

Lunch with the English

May 1959

Saroja looked out the window and saw the Morris Minor pull up in front of the small house, part of the official living quarters of her brother Rajan's textile company, Madura Coats. Rajan went outside to welcome the English couple. She followed, standing next to him stiffly. The driver stepped out to open the car door and an English woman emerged, wearing a gauzy flowered dress. Her legs were bare, perched in black pumps. Saroja couldn't see her face, which was shielded from the sun by a wide-brimmed straw hat. A man followed her out of the car, his short-sleeved white shirt gleaming in the noon sun. They each shook Rajan's hand and as the man walked over to her, Saroja straightened the folds of her sari. "How do you do? I'm Edward Cavendish," he said with a smile. She stifled the urge to put her hands together for "Namaste". Awkwardly, she reached out her right hand, not sure whether she was supposed to touch hands or give a firm grip.

She felt her hair, coiled in a bun, pulling heavily on the back of her head. On the night train from Madras she had hardly slept, arriving at five that morning. Now she felt faint and realized she hadn't eaten anything since last night.

As they went inside, Saroja noticed Mrs. Cavendish's white gloves, so incongruous in the Madurai heat. Rajan smiled and nodded for them to sit at the table. She gazed down self-consciously at the flowered table mats and at the sides of the plates, a bewildering array of forks, knives and spoons.

She had never been this close to English people. Her Anglo-Indian teachers at school had seemed exotic to her, but with enough Indian-ness to seem accessible. She heard Rajan telling the Cavendishes that she would be moving to New York in July to work in a hospital. She heard the note of pride in his voice. She imagined that when he had invited them for lunch with his sister, they had been charmed, thinking she would be shy and submissive. She saw them recalibrating, digesting that she was a doctor and going by herself to America.

Last week, after an overnight shift at the hospital and the long bus ride home, she found a postcard from Rajan waiting for her. He had been back from his textile training in Manchester for a year now and suggested that she come down to Madurai to have a meal with his English colleague and his wife. It would be good preparation for New York, he urged. "You can try out using cutlery, making conversation and eating food without spices." At first, she thought it silly to go all the way to Madurai just to have lunch. But Appa said it would be a good break from her hospital routine. He pointed out that she could visit her older sister Radha who lived in Madurai with her family.

Saroja's brother, Madurai, 1958

As she sat at the table, she wondered if Americans cared as much about table manners as the English. She looked up at Mrs. Cavendish's pale hands and thought of how at home, she would be sitting on the floor with her sisters and younger brother, eating with her right hand from a steel plate. She knew the etiquette of eating by hand – wash hands first, use the tips of your fingers of your right hand to pick up the rice and mix it with the *sambar,* a soup of lentils and vegetables with the sourness of tamarind. As far back as she could remember, she knew to serve herself with her left hand that had not touched any of the food on the plate, and never to touch anyone or anything outside her plate with her eating hand – it all came automatically. After the *sambar* there would be *rasam*, a thin broth to mix with rice. At the end would be rice and yogurt – "curds" with a lime pickle. There was the crunch of *appalam*, savoury rice flour chips, and perhaps a vegetable curry. She was used to using spoons for serving but not for eating an entire meal.

Meals at home were always vegetarian although her father was not so orthodox as to forbid his children from sampling eggs, chicken or meat outside the home. As Brahmins, "non-vegetarian" food was defiling, but she would occasionally treat herself to a chicken puff with her tea at the medical school canteen. There wasn't lingering or conversation at meal-times. After eating, they would pick up their plates and take them to the back of the house where there was a tap to rinse them and stack them. They would then return to the same room where they had eaten and pull out their books to study. Later they would unroll their bedding and it would become the communal bedroom. Saroja would move to the veranda and pour over her anatomy books, memorizing the Latin names of the body, while her sisters and younger brother slept.

Now she glanced up at Mrs. Cavendish and saw her pick up the largest spoon on the right of the plate and gently dip it into the tomato soup. She did the same, wanting to hold the spoon with her fist but then seeing how in Mrs. Cavendish's hand it was balanced delicately between her forefinger, thumb and middle finger. It felt awkward. Wasn't it much simpler to just drink out of the bowl? She picked up her spoon and thought about how at home yesterday she had nervously practiced cutting a *chapati* with a knife and fork to prepare for today.

As she sat across from Mrs. Cavendish, she wondered how it was possible to sip soup without the slightest sound – so different from how she would gulp down her *rasam* at home in Madras. Mrs. Cavendish saw her fumbling with the spoon and advised, "When you get to the end of your soup course, remember to dip your spoon away from yourself so you don't spill any on your clothes."

Saroja nodded politely in assent.

After soup, they moved on to baked cauliflower with a cream sauce. It was creamy and slightly sweet. Saroja found herself craving the tanginess of tamarind, the sharpness of ginger and the pungency of chilli. Using a fork and knife seemed cumbersome and far removed from the earthy experience of eating rice and curries with her hands. She heard Rajan telling Mr. Cavendish how much he missed fish and chips. There was a wistfulness in his voice and suddenly he was no longer the bossy older brother of her childhood, who at only thirteen took over the accounts and administration of the household. She thought about how quickly they had had to grow up with their mother Bhavani unwell and a father who travelled constantly to support a family of seven children. Bhavani drifted in and out of her own world. She would help their cook Hariharan in the kitchen, but she didn't know what they were doing in school or the challenges they were facing. If they needed two rupees for a snack after school, they had to appeal to Rajan in advance; he almost always turned down last-minute requests.

During Rajan's year away in Manchester, it was Padmini, with her organizational skills, who took on the household accounts. When a letter from Rajan arrived, Appa would read it out after dinner so they could hear about the damp and grey winter days in England when it seemed like the sun never emerged, the boiled turnips and parsnips in winter, the formalities of greetings…When Rajan described how hard it was to get out of bed and face the cold, she wondered if it was like the hill station where she had visited Radha. She remembered one visit when she had woken up in the middle of the night, the coldest she had ever been. She woke up shivering in the middle of the night. She was astonished to hear Mr. Cavendish say that New York would be even colder.

Listening to the Cavendishes' clipped accents made her realize how much more familiar England was than America. She had grown up in British India, standing beside her desk singing "God Save the King". She had watched wartime newsreels of British troops in the war, studied Shakespeare and Tennyson with Anglo-Indian teachers and read P.G. Wodehouse, Somerset Maugham, and Jane Austen. On one newsreel she saw young Princess Elizabeth being crowned when her father died. By comparison, America was remote, brash, and new. She had hardly ever seen Americans. She knew American actors like Cary Grant in *Arsenic and Old Lace* and Gregory Peck in *Roman Holiday*. She had gone to the Casino cinema in Madras to see *Roman Holiday* five times. New York evoked

Jimmy Stewart watching Grace Kelly in *Rear Window* from one New York apartment to another.

Saroja was unsure what to say to Mrs. Cavendish. "How are you adjusting to Madurai" she inquired gingerly.

"I don't know how you cope with this heat! I simply can't go out during the day" Saroja smiled. Rajan had told her that conversations with the English always came back to the weather.

When it was time for vanilla custard, she told Mrs. Cavendish how her mother would order Christmas cake from Spencer's Department Store in Madras. Rajan laughed and described how Saroja and her sister Padmini fought for the largest portion. Her brother's teasing dissolved her reticience and Saroja retorted indignantly "That wasn't me, that was Lakshman!" Their youngest brother Lakshman delighted in tormenting her. She suspected that he would miss her fury when she was gone. Thinking of him distracted her and she felt Mrs. Cavendish tapping her shoulder. "Are you nervous?"

Saroja responded "No" with surprising conviction. And it was true. She was certain that going to America was exactly the right thing to do. She was escaping other people making decisions for her – about marriage, work, children and how she would live her life.

A Long Journey

June 1959, Madras Airport

As they walked into the airport, Appa tried to take the suitcase from Saroja, but she wouldn't let go, determined to take it by herself. She held it in one hand and her carry-on bag in the other. It would be the first time she would fly on a plane. Today there was a commotion as a film star from Bombay was rushing to catch the next flight back.

Her sister Radha had been in Madras for the delivery of her baby boy and stayed on to see Saroja off, leaving three daughters and a one-month-old baby boy at home. Although only four years older than Saroja, she assumed a motherly and protective role. Like Rajan, she had had to take on more responsibility for her younger siblings and with Bhavani unable to engage with her children, it was Radha who guided Saroja as a mother would.

Saroja felt a pang when she thought of what her sister had given up. When the proposal came from Ravi for Radha, Appa was in a bind. With the pressure from his family, it was difficult to say no. Ravi needed a poised, gracious and intelligent wife to help him run a tea estate in the hills. So Appa accepted the proposal. With dedication to her younger sisters, Radha left medical school to get married. And four years later, when Saroja did well enough in chemistry and biology to have a chance to apply to medical school, it was she who went instead. If Radha had not left, Appa may not have been able to manage the fees to send Saroja to Madras Medical School.

After marrying, Radha had lived in the tea estates in the Nilgiri Mountains. She was now back in Madurai and no longer needed her handmade blue wool coat. It occupied most of the space in Saroja's suitcase and having only lived in South India, she found it hard to imagine ever needing it. The only other clothes she had were a few cotton white saris that she intended to wear at the hospital. Saroja felt both grateful and guilty to be fulfilling her sister's dream.

Suddenly she found herself fidgeting and rearranging her things. She was twenty-three and had never left her family. It slowly dawned on her that she didn't know when she could return to India. New York seemed impossibly far. She would have to change planes six times to get there.

Rajan noticed her rising anxiety and joked, "One of your planes should break down in Europe so you can have some interesting food! You must try everything they give you on the plane!" he chortled and described food she had only read about – roast meats, baked ham, fried fish, cakes… Saroja had tried Christmas cake, but had never sampled the other foods – they were forbidden for Brahmins and hard to find in Madras. But Rajan urged her to let go and sample everything – she didn't have to keep to tradition. She had no idea what that meant. What would anchor her in this new world?

From her purse, Radha pulled out a jar of lime pickle sent by her aunt, Bhavani's younger sister. Just as she placed it in Saroja's hands, Appa took it away said sternly,

"You won't need that. You are going to try new things and do whatever you need to adjust." Saroja heard this not as an admonishment. Appa was freeing her to live in a new way. He was liberating her from maintaining customs and ritual purity.

In the queue to check in, they met another woman travelling alone. Lalitha was meeting her husband in Philadelphia. She was carrying a large *veena* – a stringed musical instrument like a sitar – wrapped up in what looked like a cotton rug. Radha was happy for Saroja to have a companion, but Rajan frowned. He whispered in Saroja's ear, "Now you can't try all the food as you'll have her watching you!" Good Hindus weren't supposed to eat meat, fish and eggs – especially pious young women. It would be hard for Saroja to experiment with this woman looking over her shoulder, ready to report any straying. And if you start eating meat what next? Alcohol? Marrying foreigners?

Appa had given his consent for this move but all he could offer her was the air ticket to New York. After that, she was on her own. He didn't tell her to behave in a certain way, find a Tamil Brahmin husband or stick to what she knew. She could go to New York on her own terms. As she was leaving, Appa's eyes became moist, and he reminded her of all the marriageable boys he brought home for her to see during her first year of medical school. She had found something wrong with each one – one had uneven teeth, the other laughed too much, another was sullen.

She said with a mix of exasperation and affection "Appa, don't go on making up stories again!"

"Remember when I asked you if you wanted to be married at all? Remember what you said?" He asked.

She remembered but didn't want to say aloud, "Why did you send me to medical school if you are going to have me married off?"

But now they were all cheering for her. No one was telling her to get married.

"Once you get in, you will find your way but keep saving money," Radha said tenderly.

Saroja looked at her sister and thought about all the times she had brought her tea at night so she could study, all the ways she had comforted her when she didn't get good marks in maths. She glimpsed shadows of worry in Radha's dark eyes.

"You need to be able to come home if you have to," Radha said quietly.

Saroja embraced her sister and then clutched her father and brother's hands. Finally, she turned around, holding her carry-on and boarded the Trans World Airlines flight with Lalitha. The first stop would be Lahore. Then it was Cairo, Tehran, Beirut, Rome, Lisbon and New York – places she had read about in geography books but couldn't believe really existed.

On the sixth leg, from Lisbon to New York, the plane's engine broke down. All the passengers disembarked for the night, except the Indians. Portugal and India were in charged negotiations about the continued Portuguese occupation of Goa, so Indians were not allowed into Portugal. Finally, at midnight, a full three days after leaving Madras, the twelve Indian nationals were allowed to disembark as long as they didn't leave their hotel. Saroja climbed onto an airport bus with the others. Her first glimpse of a foreign city was Lisbon at midnight, through a bus window. She saw shop windows, cafes and cobblestone streets and longed to walk and explore. When she arrived at the hotel and was taken up to her room by the bellboy, she was astonished to see a large bowl of fruit. What luxury! She vowed to return and explore Lisbon one day.

When she arrived in New York City at Idlewild Airport, there was no one to meet her. She had sent three telegrams from Lisbon; one was to her brother Rajan: *"Your dreams have come true! Stuck in Europe!"* One was to her father: *"In Lisbon for night. Will reach a day later. All fine."* And one to her medical school classmate Siddharth: *"Arriving one day late. Same time."*. Siddharth had been in New York for a month and was the only person she knew there. Would he meet her?

The immigration officer asked for her letter of invitation from the hospital and after glancing at it waved her through. Glass doors she didn't realize were there parted on their own and she saw women wearing summer dresses and hats and Men in suits with their ties loosened. They were carefully inspecting every arriving passenger for the person they had come to welcome. No one in a sari and no one with dark skin except the Black men wheeling the luggage. She didn't see Siddharth.

She worried how she would get to Brooklyn. She asked for help at the information desk, and a kindly woman showed her how to put a coin in the payphone to call the hospital. After putting her on hold for a few minutes, the hospital receptionist said said she could take a taxi and the hospital would reimburse her this one time.

When she stepped outside the searing heat stunned her. She never imagined New York could be as hot as India. It was 8 pm and still light outside! In Madras it would be pitch black by 6:30 in the evening.

She went to the taxi stand and got into a yellow cab. The driver's English sounded rough and nasal. She climbed in and took in the smell of stale cigarettes. He put her suitcase in the back and looked at her sari, asking if she was from India.

"I don't mind Indians, but your country is too friendly to the Russians!" he said, as they drove from Queens to Brooklyn. In the distance, she saw the East River, the Empire State Building and the UN. It was so huge and grand but then the roads had more holes in them, the houses were shabby and run down and there were men outside bars in the July evening. The area around the airport was white and as they got close to the hospital in Crown Heights, the people outside drinking and chatting on this summer evening were dark skinned. This New York was not the sterile city she had pictured at the US Information Centre in Madras. She brimmed with excitement, almost forgetting her disappointment that Siddharth hadn't come to meet her.

Confronting Race

New York, March 1960

Saroja wearily pushed open the hospital door after her night shift. It was eight months since that muggy July evening when she landed in New York. She smiled wanly during the breaks between patients, grimacing from the cold, as the American nurses cheerily proclaimed, "Spring is around the corner, Dr. Saroja!" It was late March, yet the bracing wind made her face sting. She turned around and went back inside to get a coffee to fortify herself to walk the two blocks to the female doctors' residence.

She had arrived just a month ago from Brooklyn, getting into NYU's coveted paediatrics residency program. Bellevue Hospital was in an area on East 21st St. that was mostly Puerto Rican. Saroja felt like she was back in India, dealing with failure to thrive, worms in children and tropical illnesses. All hospital staff had to learn medical Spanish and most of the time she had interpreters with her.

When she reached the vending machines, she found other residents there, from the Philippines, Pakistan, Iran, Egypt, Argentina, New Zealand and South Africa. About a third were women, the same proportion as in her graduating class at Madras Medical School. Several of her professors had also been women. She had thought the U.S. would be so advanced and was taken aback to see that while American women were nurses, they were rarely doctors. It was hard to befriend the nurses as they tended to see the female doctors as competition in the race to snare a doctor husband. As a result, almost all her friends were also foreigners.

The American staff found most foreign accents impenetrable but somehow, they understood her. She was often called on to "translate" the English of Lucia from Argentina and even for Patrick from New Zealand. She had never imagined that speaking English would be an advantage in America.

"Saroja, aren't you done with your shift?" called out Belen. Belen was Filipina, always dressed in a fashionable dress that she had sewn herself. Like the other Filipina women doctors, Belen was at ease with American culture and exuberantly expressive. She would make chicken adobo on her off days on the small burner at the end of their floor, singing and dancing in the hallway with abandon.

"I need a coffee for the walk back to the hostel," Saroja said wearily, using the Indian/British word instead of the more common "dorm" in American English. She dropped a dime into the machine and waited for the paper cup to fill. She longed for the rich and flavourful coffee of South India. She took a sip and remembered her news.

"I'm going to Iowa on Saturday!" Saroja announced to the staff around her.

"Who are you visiting?" asked Rabia, a doctor from Islamabad and the first Pakistani Saroja had ever met. She had cooked a fragrant biryani in their dorm the previous weekend.

"I have a cousin in India whose brother-in-law is an astrophysicist at the University of Iowa. He says Iowa is nothing like New York and I should see it. I will stop in St Louis on the way and see my friend Geeta from medical school."

"What is the route?" asked Dr Annie, from Manila.

American geography and history had been entirely absent from Saroja's British colonial education, so she guessed.

"Maryland, Virginia, Kentucky…" she pronounced it "*Ken* ticky," accenting the first syllable. The state names seemed fanciful, lacking the solidity of real places.

Walter, the Afrikaner physician from Capetown, South Africa suddenly looked up. He came over and said with concern,

"You need to be careful when you go through the South. There is segregation." He paused.

"Remember the sit-ins at the lunch counters at Woolworths in Greensboro last month? There is violence there for anyone who looks…"

His voice trailed off.

Saroja remembered walking through the same lounge a few weeks before and seeing the TV news about a sit-in in North Carolina aimed at integrating lunch counters. It had seemed distant and removed from her life in New York. Now she realized she could be mistaken for Black. Her shoulders tensed. In India she had seen people shunning "untouchable" castes, but it was not something her family believed in or practiced. She had never considered what it would be to experience such exclusion herself. Why hadn't any of the Americans told her about these risks? She was grateful to Walter and thought ruefully that it was a South African, not an American, who warned her about segregation in the U.S.

The next day was her day off to get ready for the trip but first, she had a visit to make. Soon after waking up, she went to the corner store to buy some oranges to take to Jaya and Seshadri. Seshadri was a medical school classmate who had come to work in Harlem the year before. Unlike the rest of them, he was married. His wife Jaya was only 18 and had just had a baby. They lived on his meagre salary from Knickerbocker Hospital, in a walk-up near 14th Street. It was Seshadri who had persuaded both Siddharth and Shamsuddin to work at Knickerbocker Hospital where they felt exploited as foreign doctors.

Saroja in Baltimore, 1961

Jaya and Seshadri were generous despite having very little themselves, and always invited Saroja to come for a South Indian meal on her day off. Seshadri wanted Jaya to have company as she was isolated in a strange culture with a baby in their small apartment. Saroja found it touching that Siddharth would offer to watch the baby on his nights off so the young couple could go out for a movie.

Seshadri's older brother Raman lived nearby. He had a good job as a chemist and had left his wife and son in India, so he came over for evening meals to his brother and sister-in-law's apartment. Instead of being grateful for their hospitality, he was rude and insulting – criticizing his brother's decisions over the household and Jaya's cooking.

When Saroja arrived with her oranges she found Siddharth with Seshadri and Jaya in the kitchen washing dishes. The men had already eaten lunch and Jaya was waiting to eat with Saroja. Siddharth held the baby, laughing. As soon as Raman came in, he barked for his food to be served. He saw the bottle of sweet green hot dog relish that Siddharth had brought as a gift for the meal. Raman took the bottle and hurled it into the garbage. There was utter silence and Raman left after he finished his meal. As soon as he was safely gone, Siddharth did an impression of Raman throwing the relish bottle that made them erupt in peals of laughter. Saroja didn't know what was more amusing, Siddharth's imitation of Raman or that his idea of a house gift was hot dog relish.

After lunch, Siddharth walked her to the subway and took her back to Brooklyn before taking the train all the way back north to Harlem. They talked to each other about their families, sometimes continuing on the hall phone late at night. Saroja had long forgiven Siddharth for not coming to the airport that day she arrived in New York. There were so many buses and trains to take from Harlem to where the airport was in Queens; he arrived after she had already left. He despondently returned home with the flowers he had extravagantly purchased for her. Now when they met in New York on their days off, they would see a movie at Radio City Music Hall and have a twenty-five cent slice of pizza. In India, they might not have even met, but in New York they had a bond built on coming from the same place and going through the same adventure.

Siddharth's childhood and upbringing were starkly different from Saroja's. His first language was Hindi, not Tamil, as his father worked for the British administration in North India. He went away to boarding school when he was only seven and didn't grow up with his brothers. He learned Tamil at fifteen when his family moved to South India, so he spoke it without nuance, mixing street slang and formal expressions. Despite being Tamilian, sometimes he would fall into North Indian stereotypes and make derogatory comments about South Indians. She would bristle in those moments and get angry with him only to relax when he made another joke.

The next morning, she took the subway from Atlantic Ave. to Port Authority Bus Terminal to board the Greyhound bus. On the first night, she got off at a stop and saw "white" and "coloured" signs posted at the women's restrooms. She looked around and saw no one, so she used the one for whites without knowing where she fit in. During the trip, she was not treated badly but was always aware of her exoticism. Sometimes at the rest stops American tourists asked to take their pictures with her, as with a strange landmark.

Siddharth was going to a surgical conference in Chicago when Saroja was in Iowa so she arranged to stop and meet him there on her way back. They would travel back to New York together. For Siddharth, being male and dark-skinned was more challenging.. Soon after arriving in the U.S., he took a bus to Virginia for a medical conference. When he got out at a rest stop to use a water fountain the local police approached him for using a "whites-only" water fountain. Until then he hadn't known about "separate but equal" facilities, nor that he would be seen as a Black man. The grandson of an economics professor and the son of a Cambridge University graduate, Siddharth was at ease with the elite. He was angry to be treated as a second-class citizen.

Siddharth and Saroja were novelties in the U.S. at a time when there were hardly any Indians. In 1960, there were about 45,000 Indians in the entire U.S., less than 0.5 percent of the foreign-born population.

In New York, the patients they treated were Black, white and occasionally Puerto Rican. With her caramel skin, my mother was frequently mistaken for Puerto Rican. In Harlem, my father's mannerisms and accent labelled him as a foreigner but as on the Virginia trip, he was mistaken for Black when he ventured south. On a trip to Baltimore in 1961, he was turned away at a barbershop, not realizing he had broken the code and entered a white area.

After a year, Siddharth got fed up with the poor working conditions at his hospital in Harlem and applied to do a Ph.D. in Anatomy, thinking that would bring him closer to his dream of qualifying as a surgeon. He got a scholarship to Jefferson Medical School in Philadelphia and by the end of 1960 moved there.

It was during one of Saroja's visits to Philadelphia that they decided to get married. When they told Raman and Noser, Siddharth's Gujarati roommates, their new friends prepared a *kheer* with rice, milk, sugar and saffron. Breaking the news to their parents was more complicated. It was unorthodox to *tell* your parents you were getting married, as opposed to *asking*. Phoning was out of the question. Saroja's family didn't have a phone. Siddharth's family had a phone but calls were so expensive that after shouting greetings it was time to get off. So, they each sent a blue aerogramme to their families.

It took three weeks for a letter to reach India and for a reply to arrive. They waited patiently. Saroja's father Arunachalam replied first. He had gone to meet Siddharth's family at their house at Mount Road and was impressed with their education and prominence. He gave the couple his blessings, saying he couldn't have chosen a better match. He said he would be fine with any type of wedding they wanted, even a simple civil ceremony was fine. Saroja told Siddharth this was typical of her father, who had little patience with excessive religiosity and rituals. Siddharth's mother's letter came a few days later. Kalpakam was clearly disappointed they couldn't come to India for the wedding. Given that was out of the question, she insisted they find a Hindu priest. There was no question of any family from India coming for the wedding. Foreign exchange was hard to come by and the cost was exorbitant.

Locating a Hindu priest was not simple. Saroja wrote to her childhood friend Uma, who had moved to Washington DC, to see if the Indian diplomatic community there knew of anyone. Uma eventually found a priest who could perform the rituals in Sanskrit at a church in Maryland. They went to Washington for a simple ceremony after which Uma and her husband hosted a dinner at home for them.

Saroja felt sad to have no family at the wedding – no sisters, brothers, parents, aunts or uncles. At least she had Uma to give her a hug. One of the few photos she had already hung up in their new apartment was of the reception dinner in Uma's house in Washington. Saroja is wearing a gleaming platinum silk sari with a green brocade blouse, laughing as she breaks an *"appalam"* over Siddharth's head, a traditional ritual of a bride and groom.

After their marriage in 1961, they both moved to Baltimore, which while not exactly in the South, had elements of Southern segregation. Saroja was working as a paediatrician at a University of Maryland-affiliated hospital and was shocked to find separate wards for black and white children, with the white children in far superior facilities. My father worked in another Baltimore hospital treating victims of stab wounds and drug overdoses, and first-hand saw that black Americans lived in a world with inferior resources and services.

They were familiar with discrimination and government attempts to rectify it. In Tamil Nadu, their home state, the state government had instituted reservation systems in the 1950s for government jobs and university admissions, to rectify the British tendency to favour Brahmins in administrative jobs. The quotas for Brahmins were restricted as a result. Of course, caste discrimination continued in other insidious ways, but for them, caste separation was hopelessly old-fashioned and backwards. America represented everything that was modern, so it was a shock to see the US maintaining similar, descent-based barriers.

These windows into racial separations in the U.S. helped Saroja to understand the urgency of the civil rights movement. After long hospital shifts, she would watch TV news coverage of the Freedom Riders, activists' murders, bombings of churches, demonstrations and marches. Martin Luther King's nonviolent tactics were familiar to her, evoking her earliest memories of Gandhi and the "Quit India" movement.

Despite being patronized and often professionally underestimated, Saroja and Siddharth knew that the discrimination they faced in the US was nothing compared to the racism that oppressed Black Americans. It was strange to live with the duality of privilege (doctors, from highly educated families, with aspirations) and low status (salaries low enough to qualify for housing projects, prejudice against dark skin, not belonging to mainstream American professional society).

Saroja and Siddharth, Philadelphia, 1962

Dead or Alive?

February 2011, London

On a dreary and dark February afternoon I was in the kitchen making dinner while the children played in the living room down the hall. At 4 and 2, Leela and Kailash needed supervision, but the kitchen was in a far corner of the Victorian flat with its cumbersome layout designed for a different era. I left them to play on their own as I heated up vegetable soup in the kitchen. As I stirred the pot, I heard screaming. I resolved to leave them to solve the conflict on their own. It was less than a year since I had left a busy professional life in New York to be a stay-at-home mother. I was still finding my way.

Leela raced to the kitchen yelling "Mommy! Mommy!" Her face was contorted with worry, so distraught it was hard for her to speak. "Come! It's Kailash!"

I ran after her into the living room. I couldn't make sense of what I was seeing. A tall standing lamp had fallen on the floor, Kailash's small body had collapsed next to it, his right hand splayed out and charred black. I could smell burning and when I looked down, to my horror I realized that the burning was his flesh. He was absolutely still.

What had happened? It didn't make any sense. Leela explained that they had been playing with the lamp. But how would a lamp knock a child out? To my relief, he suddenly started screaming with pain so he was alive! Relief turned to panic. Leela needed me to be a tower of strength. I had no idea what to do. I am nothing like my parents.

With shaking hands I called "999". Time stood still while we waited. Kailash screamed for Daddy. I wished I could turn back time. Why did we even that faulty lamp?

The ambulance team, a trio headed by a Scottish woman and two men, were comforting. The woman spoke with a tender smile, "And how are you doing?"

I was speechless, in shock. My doctor parents had always navigated illnesses and emergencies. Now I desperately missed my mother's steely calm.

August 1969, New York City

On my last day in North America, I spend most of my time outside playing with my cousin Harsha. We race up and down the slides and run through the water fountain to cool off in the humid August New York heat. Finally, my aunt says it is time to go inside and we skip out of the playground to take the elevator up to the apartment in Lefrak City.

My mother, father, one-year-old sister Meera and I are in New York City staying with my uncle, aunt and cousin until our flight to India the next day. Three days before, we had come by ship from Halifax, Nova Scotia. After a decade of limited prospects in North America, my parents have decided to move back to India. I am five years old and all I know of the world is eastern Canada.

Harsha and I chase each other down the hall and tumble inside the open door. My parents are hunched over my sister Meera, who is on the floor, limp and motionless. My parents look at my aunt wordlessly. Why is no one talking? "Is Meera dead?" I ask and immediately it hits too close to home. My mother explains that Meera has fallen and suffered a concussion. I don't understand. We are getting on the plane to India tomorrow; how we will manage?

When I asked my mother more than fifty years later to describe the experience, there is no dramatic story. It is characteristic of her to stick to the facts and keep the emotions at bay. She describes a hot summer evening in a sweltering apartment. She gives my sister a bath in an attempt to cool her down. She puts the baby on a low sofa and turns around for a split second to get a diaper. My sister rolls over and onto the floor, losing consciousness. She and my father take Meera in a taxi to St John's Hospital on Queens Boulevard. It is the night before we are to leave for India, so they discuss possibly cancelling the flight. They don't know how long it will take before they know how serious the diagnosis is.

During the taxi ride Meera wakes up so when they arrive at the hospital, they have a skull x-ray taken. The doctors emerge to say there is no damage, but they warn that children's skull bones are pliable, so damages don't always show up. They advise to keep Meera at the hospital overnight for observation, but my mother refuses. She is certain she can monitor Meera. The hospital makes them sign a form "Discharged against medical advice." My mother does not panic and calms down my worried father. They return back to the apartment at Lefrak City.

Saroja stays up all night with Meera, listening to her heart and looking at her pupils every half hour to see signs of bleeding in the brain. Finally, in the early morning, she collapses with exhaustion only to be woken up by Meera climbing over her. Meera is fine.

The preternatural calm is and always has been Saroja, my mother.

October 2020, Costa Rica and Haverford, Pennsylvania

Saroja's voice brims over with warmth and exuberance to hear his voice. "Hi Kailash," she laughs. "I was wondering when you would call." He is a bit late tonight.

"Sorry, Paati. I had homework."

She asks her usual question but seems distracted

"What's new?"

"Nothing much. I have to do my homework and online school is boring. What are you watching?"

He can see she is looking at something.

She laughs with delight "I'm watching a very good movie! I don't know if it's suitable for you…"

"When your mother was small, I used to take her to a community cinema which showed foreign films and art films. I went so often that they named a chair after me!"

"What's it called, Paati?"

"*Queen and Slim.*"

"Paati wanted to watch the movie, so we didn't talk much," later Kailash tells me with disappointment.

I look up the movie. It is about a young Black couple who are persecuted by the police and end up killing someone in self-defence. It is directed by an African American woman director who explores race, gender and sexuality.

Later I explain to Kailash: "That is exactly the kind of movie Paati likes."

Reflection

November 2020

"The U.S. is not what it was," my mother says to me over the phone.

"What do you mean?" I ask

"It's not the place I found when I first came, a place that welcomed someone like me and gave me chances I would have never had in India. People are struggling here too now."

"How do you feel about being an American now? Are you glad you came?"

"Oh, of course. I could never have succeeded in India the way I did here. Yes, there was discrimination, but it would have been worse in India, and I didn't have the connections to do well there. In India, I would have been nothing special. In the U.S. people paid attention to me. I was a novelty. Being female and young helped and when I did my work well, I was recognized."

Unlike my mother, I did not earn my nationality. It came to me by birth. I am American but after many years living outside the U.S., ambivalently so. I do not support the direction of American democracy and the distortions of a wealthy country willing to tolerate child poverty, violence and injustice. My mother sees these flaws but appreciates what she was able to accomplish that would have been closed to her in India. I take those privileges for granted.

I came to motherhood in my 40s, much later than my mother. I have been able to take time away from work to be with my children and to choose the assignments I want. I see the joy and also the drudgery of motherhood and when I miss my work my mother says "Veena, you are doing important work now. The children need you. You are a good mother."

She does not easily give compliments so this is a profound gift.

My life is as different from my mother's as hers was from her own mother Bhavani's. I married at 41 and have navigated many cultures and countries, never fully belonging to any. Yet when everything is scraped away, we share the belief that connection is possible across cultures. Saroja's explorations and intrepid spirit built the scaffolding for my sister and me to experiment and find our own scaffoldings. She has left this legacy for us.

THE WILLOW BOX

Kumi Konno

Japan

Introduction:

I told my mother that I was going to write about the lives of our mothers with friends. Surprisingly, she agreed to tell me her life story with a twinkle in her eye, asking if I really would write in English. More than anything else, she said, she wanted to know about the lives of other women who lived in the same era. My mother's interest helped our conversation begin smoothly. It was a challenge for me as I had never dared before to engage with my mother's emotional side. My writing was slow because a nuance in Japanese could not be transformed into English by mere translation. I shifted between the two languages, which are completely different in nature. This process led me to discover her as a woman in her own right. My mother seemed happy to share her memories, which she might not have told without this project. While writing, I realized that the sorrows and pains we have in our lives can transform into something different, something called love, over time. I feel fortunate to have had this opportunity while my mother is alive.

A call

It is a scary time, it is not the first time. Fear is invisible. For days, I wake up early. It is still dark outside. I walk down to the kitchen and wash coffee cups left from last night while putting a kettle on.

The virus has shrunk both lives and minds. We are all nervous wearing face masks. The government shut schools, museums, libraries, and places where people gather. They tell us we should avoid unnecessary outings. Day by day, it gets gloomier. On the street, people talk to one another, "We don't know how it goes", "It is frightening" as in the time of the nuclear accident in Fukushima.

I grind coffee beans and set a filter. Pouring hot water slowly, making a circular movement. The aroma of freshly made coffee is full throughout the room now. I sit at a corner of the dining table and sip coffee. Caffeine immediately stimulates my nerves. I breathe deeply and say to myself: "I will call my mother." Since the outbreak of the virus, I have been thinking about her a lot.

I wait until 8 a.m. to call her. She picks up the phone after six rings.

"How are you doing, Mum?"

"I am doing so-so, but my body is stiff."

"Mum, it is a psychological thing. We are all the same."

"I rarely go out to central Tokyo. But now we are told not to go to shopping areas, I feel so restricted."

"I know, but at least you are not isolated. We can always talk on the phone, can't we? And if you want, I will visit you. I mean if you are not nervous."

"Of course not, you can come anytime, unless you don't mind taking the bus and train."

"Mum, I still go on the train for meetings when I have to. Don't worry."

"When are you coming?"

"I am supposed to attend a meeting tomorrow, but I think it is going to be cancelled. Could I call you tomorrow morning again?"

"Of course. I have nothing on tomorrow, the day after tomorrow and so on."

We both laugh.

I put the phone down and look out of the window. The sky is now clear. The outline of the roofs makes geometric shapes against the deep blue background. I have seen this picture for many years. And today, it looks different, sharp, cold and somehow surrealistic. I suddenly feel uneasy about tomorrow. If tomorrow doesn't come, how would I live today? I don't think it is an outrageous imagination.

A call again

Next morning, I wake up and walk to the window to open the sliding shutter. On the white wall of the house across the street, light is already reflecting. It is going to be a sunny day. From the veranda, I look at the tall tree in the neighbour's garden. It was there when we moved into this house more than twenty years ago. Every year, the morning after a typhoon passed, I saw it standing with dignity. Its stillness amazed me. It is fulfilled with what it has and takes everything that comes.

I sit down at a small desk beside the bed and check the news. The spread of Coronavirus infection covers the top news and a discussion about Tokyo Olympics follows. But now - Olympics this summer? How unrealistic it sounds.

After sending emails to the people I was supposed to meet, I look up at the clock. It is already half-past eight. I press her number on my iPhone. She picks up the phone almost immediately after the first ring.

"Hello?"

"Hi, Mum, it is me."

"I know it is you. Are you coming today?"

"Yes, can I come early? It seems I have nothing on today."

"Of course!" Her tone is high today.

"Mum, you talked about the old family photos. Are they still there?"

"Yes, they are upstairs. I have meant to sort them out for long, but I haven't done so yet."

"Could I have a look today? I was always curious about them."

"Yes, but so many photos are jumbled together. I hope you won't be surprised."

"No, I won't. I can leave soon, so will be with you within an hour, OK?"

"I am waiting."

I walk down to the kitchen and take a new packet of coffee for her. She loves hand-roasted coffee from my local shop. I put it in my bag. I knew of the existence of the old photos as she had mentioned them in the past. I had ignored what she said, unconcernedly. I didn't want to be sentimental about those who were gone, but it was not the only reason. There is something about her early life.

Albums

I ring the doorbell at her house in Tanashi, a suburb town in the western portion of Tokyo. More than sixty years ago, my grandmother, Tsuma, bought a piece of land and built a wooden house. My parents started their married life there with her. Since the death of my father, my mother has maintained the house and lived with my younger sister.

She opens the door with a big smile.

"Come in."

"Thank you. It is such a nice day."

"Isn't it? I have hung a lot of washing this morning."

She leads me to the living room and asks me what I would like to have. She usually serves Japanese tea first. Her living room is colourful, a mixture of many things, nothing valuable but all that she cherishes. On the wall, there hangs a red rag with a geometric pattern from Afghanistan next to the green painted paper mask my elder son made almost twenty years ago.

"A strange atmosphere, isn't it? The TV news says Ginza is almost a ghost town after ten p.m." she says.

"I know people rush home after work. We are all very nervous."

I look out at the garden from the living room. It is so small that I can reach the back wall within twenty steps. I haven't noticed that until now. When I was a child, everything around me felt a lot bigger.

She serves me tea in an old ceramic bowl that belonged to Tsuma. A round tea bowl that fits in the palms. It has a motif of a sitting Buddhist monk in a red robe.

"I remember this motif, so skilfully drawn," I say.

"Since you have come, I took it from the cupboard. This is Kutani ware. In those days, a peddler from the north part of Japan would travel to Kagoshima, the very south part, to sell these things. Such a long distance, isn't it amazing?"

I look at the monk's severe face, sip the green tea and put it down on the table.

"Mum, I've been recalling the Fukushima nuclear disaster. The atmosphere was similar, don't you think?"

"That was frightening. It seems a long time ago."

It was nine years ago. The accident is weighing on us, and now we confront Coronavirus.

I say, "I was on the phone with my friend the other day. She said, 'We are the rare generation who have experienced, the nuclear plant explosion, Tsunami, series of earthquakes, unprecedented destructive typhoons and now Coronavirus. What we haven't had yet is a world war.' But your generation experienced WW2."

She nods while sipping tea.

Holding a small bowl half-filled with green tea, I say to her:

"Can I see the photos now?"

"Yes, but there is no heating upstairs. I hope you are okay."

Every time I visit her house, I feel the absence of my father. Since his death, my mother hasn't changed anything upstairs, which consists of two rooms. The room which is twelve tatami mats in size is a bedroom and was my father's study. The other room of six tatami mats was once my room where now my mother stores everything from the past.

I walk upstairs. She follows and says, "It is in Oshi-ire in the six tatami mats room." The sound of Oshi-ire, a built-in closet, brings a nostalgic feel. I go straight to Oshi-ire, open and look into its depth. I remember we put futons (1) and other seasonal goods there. It is big enough for a small child to hide, and so I did when I wanted to be alone in the darkness. Now it is packed with boxes of different sizes, leaving no space for anything.

I start to pull out boxes from the front. Behind my back, my mother points out an old container woven from willow fibre. I pull the willow box out slowly. I open the lid. There are a tremendous number of photos almost overflowing from the container. At a glance, they are from various eras.

"There should be albums, underneath all the photos," she says. It is going to be an excavation.

I dig inside the box and touch the edge of a bound book. There are several at the bottom. I take out the sunken albums. They are all hard-covered with fabric.

Kanesuke and Tsuma

I open the dark navy album. Inside, the colour of the album mount is faded and the photos are almost yellow. On the first page, there are photos of two different couples. One is with a young woman in Kimono holding her baby. Next to her, a young man in a three-piece suit is standing. They look like they are in their late twenties. I don't know them. Another is a photo of a much older couple, at least fifteen years or more. A woman in Kimono is sitting on a chair and a man stands beside her with a dog. This woman with a long face and a big-boned body, I can trace it is young Tsuma, my grandmother. And the man must be her husband, whom I didn't meet. But who are the young couple? I stare at the photo. My mother stretches her hand from behind and touches the baby with her forefinger.

"It is me."

I look back at her.

"Are they your real parents?"

"Yes, and she is my mother."

I look at the photo again to search for any resemblance between the woman and my mother. They both have a roundish face frame, but otherwise, I can't find any similarities.

She doesn't remove her finger from the photo until I say, "I didn't know you had their photo."

I put it down and take out another old album made with dark green fabric. On the first page, there is a photo of my mother and my paternal grandmother Sayo sitting at a veranda. It was taken just before her marriage. She almost looks like a teenager, charming and so relaxed with Sayo, her future mother-in-law. I am confused. Had she ever been at ease with Sayo? I can only recall my mother looking tense whenever Sayo was around. If her married life started like this, what made her change so much afterwards?

I turn the page. There is a gap between the years from the previous page. A series of small photos are laid out in order.

"Oh look, it is you with Sayo and your uncle," she points out the photo. There, three of us, me around four years old, Sayo and behind us my uncle standing. We are in a stand, probably in a baseball stadium. I look like a curious little one with large eyes fully opened and seem excited to be there. My uncle is in his casual suit looking relaxed and Sayo is smiling. We are enjoying a day out together.

"Did she ever smile?" I ask her.

In the photo, Sayo looks different from how I remember her.

My mother looks at it and says after a pause, "There must be a time she enjoyed."

I close the album and pick up photos randomly from the willow box. I continue and continue like a card game, take one, observe it, put it down and take another. Then I stop. They don't match the images in my memory. I breathe deeply. I am overwhelmed by the thought that I could have misunderstood my family entirely. Beside me, my mother picks up a photo and says, "Look, it is rare, you are with two grandmothers. Who took this photo?" Both grandmothers, Sayo and Tsuma are in kimono standing straight in front of a sizeable Western-style building. Between them, I am in a white shirt and a skirt of dark colour.

She continues, "I wonder where you all went."

I have no idea at all. And I start to feel I can't take any more.

She looks at me and says, "Oh, it is nearly one. Would you like to eat noodles? I can make some quickly."

We come down to the dining room together.

"You can always come back to look at them. I will leave the photos as they are. We don't use the room anyway."

I nod with a smile, trying to hide my perturbation.

From the kitchen, she brings a steaming bowl of Udon (2) and other small dishes which she calls leftovers from yesterday. In a bowl, a whole boiled egg with cooked vegetables sits on a bed of noodles. I hold the warm bowl and smell the traditional stock of dried small sardines. She still cooks very well. The tasty broth warms up my body. After lunch, I make coffee with the beans I have brought. She puts the TV on, and we watch an afternoon program together.

In the photos, our family, all people I know, looks different. At the stadium, I am an innocent child, a loved one. And my mother, in her twenties, is pretty and hopeful. Did she lose her brightness after her marriage? Or didn't she change at all? Have I looked at her with a biased view for years? My perception of her as a stressed wife is rooted in the time we lived with my grandmothers. I don't want to look back at that time as it could evoke uneasiness between us.

Facts

Every time I think of my mother, I feel a little guilt. For considerable years of my early life, I thought I would never want to be like her. I remembered her as a young woman looking constantly stressed. But now, the aged photo of her biological parents has brought me a much larger time frame of her life which I didn't know. What she says about her biological family, the adoption, her life with new parents, the war and her married life is like unfolding a picture scroll.

Sadako, my mother, was born on November 29, 1935, in Kofu, the capital city of Yamanashi prefecture adjacent to Tokyo, in a middle-class family. Her father was a public servant formerly a son of a successful wholesale merchant of Japanese split-toe socks. When Sadako was four years old, her mother died. Soon, she was adopted by a distant relative in Kagoshima, the very southernmost part of Kyushu. There, she started a new life with Kanesuke and his wife Tsuma.

After the sudden death of Kanesuke, she was raised by Tsuma, and both survived WW2. Sadako studied at a university in Tokyo and married my father, Hiroshi, who was the son of Tsuma's elder sister, Sayo. They had two daughters, my younger sister and I, and lived in a suburb of Tokyo. Since my father's death, she has been a widow. She is now eighty-four and a grandmother of two boys.

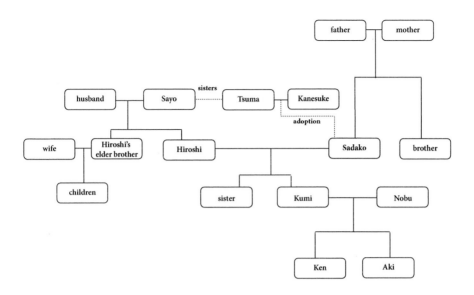

My mother kept the adoption secret from me while Tsuma was alive. I never asked about her biological parents. For us, the family lineage always meant my father's side as Sayo and Tsuma were sisters. My mother's side has stayed blank. I now wonder how she felt about that. Did she feel isolated? Or maybe, she didn't want to be touched?

From home, I text her.

"Thank you for the noodles, so delicious. The old albums are amazing. Could I come again? I want to see more."

After a few minutes, she texts back.

"I'm glad you came. I start to remember many things now. And thank you for the coffee. You don't need to bring things every time you come."

A second visit to the willow box

Today, my mother is more talkative. She says after my visit, the memory of her life in Yamanashi came back. She starts to talk about her biological mother.

"My mother was good with her hands. The neighbours asked her to make Kimono. There were always beautiful silk textiles at home. I remember their colours."

The family occasionally went out to dine at the restaurant in the department store in Kofu.

"I clearly remember the pair of black enamel shoes that I wore then. I was so excited to dine there with my family." In the late 1930s, eating out at a restaurant was very special.

"And another scene I remember is the bakery shop. I was on my mother's back and looking at my favourite chocolate pastries displayed in the glass case. When I cried too much, she took me there. She knew I would stop crying if I had one."

My mother looks happy with her dreamy eyes.

"Oh, you were spoiled." I smile back to her.

The country was heading towards WW2 and life was becoming tougher for ordinary people. After her mother's death, their relatives suggested that her father remarry and foster Sadako to Kanesuke. When Tsuma came to take Sadako, she didn't resist. Her only sibling, an older brother, stayed with the family and saw Sadako leave. She never talks about the separation scene. She says, "I remember happy things before my mother's death, but hardly anything after that."

"Don't you remember anything about your brother?" I ask her, hesitating.

"It is strange, isn't it? I don't remember anything about him. Maybe, I have unconsciously buried things I couldn't help."

From Yamanashi, Tsuma and Sadako travelled to the South, some 1250 km by changing trains and a ferry to Kagoshima. My mother remembers the time she was about to cross the Kanmon straits, separating the mainland of Japan from Kyusyu.

"The ferry looked enormous. I knew I had to get on." It was her farewell to the mainland. Apart from the Kanmon straits, her memory of the journey is extremely blurred.

At home in Kajiki, a town in Kagoshima, Kanesuke was waiting for them. He was a mild-natured, retired journalist. Tsuma who had worked in the Bank of Taiwan in Taipei before WW2 was far from a typical Japanese housewife who served her husband. At home, Kanesuke was more capable of carrying out household duties than Tsuma. They had no children.

My mother says, "Their house was an ordinary Japanese house, but the interior was modern. I remember thinking it was a nice house." Although Kajiki was far south from Kofu, she didn't feel she had come to a strange place.

"Kanesuke loved fishing and owned a beautifully made fishnet. And he really had a good aesthetic sense. He selected everything they had at home. And the chic kimono and accessories Tsuma wore when she went out, those were from him."

However, death took away another parent from Sadako. After two years, Kanesuke died of a cerebral infarction. His death left Tsuma and Sadako alone to live through the wartime. Sadako only remembers his grand funeral.

School life under the shadow of totalitarian militarism was all about national discipline. My mother remembers students bowed towards a Ho-an-den every morning, a small shrine-like building installed on the elementary school premises. It housed the photographs of the incumbent Emperor and Empress and a copy of the Imperial Rescript of Education that preached universal morality of Japanese subjects.

In the classroom, most of the study time was spent reading the Imperial Rescript of Education aloud.

"Students who memorized the rescript quickly and accurately were praised. We children had no clue of the real meaning."

Sadako in the time of elementary school

Being a small girl, Sadako didn't participate in war training. In Kagoshima, thanks to native vegetables and seafood from the nearby sea, they never experienced starvation like people in big cities. However, food such as rice, miso and sugar were supplied only occasionally. People queued each time there was a notice for distribution.

Kajiki was near the Kanoya airbase and Sadako saw American planes flying over often. They shot civilians, including small children sporadically. Every day there were casualties on the streets.

"There was a large hospital near the school. Those who were shot by the Americans were carried there. I passed the hospital and heard the crying of injured people. I felt that the American air force was shooting us for fun, just like a game. That was the scariest thing."

Tsuma hardly talked about the past. But there was one thing, and only once she talked about the day of the Kajiki air raid to me. Her story was emotional and brief but my mother remembers the day clearly.

Kajiki air raid

It was August 11 in 1945, only three days before Japan's Acceptance of the Potsdam Declaration. (3) The country was in a desperate state, but people who had no information about the facts of the war situation were carrying out their daily lives.

It was hot from the morning and Tsuma had workers in the garden. She remembered it was a distribution day for Takuan, pickled radish, and asked Sadako to go to the distribution place in the town centre.

Around half-past ten, when Sadako walked halfway, she heard the sound of planes. This time, it was not a few. There were an immense number of fighter planes in the sky. They soon started to shoot down. She hid herself and walked underneath the eaves. After a few steps, she felt a bullet passing just beside her left ear. A sharp impulse penetrated her nerves. She went into the nearby large house of a merchant. Once she ran into the house, she saw a middle-aged navy officer standing on the earthen floor alone. The house was used as lodging for high officers. The officer said to her it was dangerous to be there as the American would target it. He took her hand and got out of the house but Sadako could not run at his speed. He then held her in his arms to run. Above his big shoulders, she saw many planes – all seemed to be aiming at them. There were explosive noises and crying. After having run a considerable distance, they had a narrow escape. They reached the riverside to hide under a bamboo bush. She crouched down with him. For how long, she doesn't remember. When the roar of fighter planes stopped, they slowly stood up and looked back to the town. What they saw was only smoke and fire. Without a word, the officer pulled her hand and slowly walked back, passing the devastating scenes, burning houses. When they returned to the large house, it was on fire, half burned down. There Sadako left him. She doesn't remember if they conversed.

"I don't even remember if I said 'Thank you' to him. I really hope I did."

The town looked utterly destroyed. She walked towards her home. The area up to the Hachiman shrine was completely burned down. Almost like a miracle, the tall trees in the shrine park had stopped the fire. All the houses beyond the park looked intact. She started to run. Her home was still standing. Inside, Tsuma who had given up hope for Sadako screamed to see her alive. Tsuma held Sadako firmly, crying and repeating, "I thought you had been killed," again and again.

On that day, eighteen U.S. military planes threw down incendiaries and mopped up what was left with machine guns. A total of 650000 m2 was destroyed by fire, and twenty-six people including fifteen students of Junior High School were killed. A large area of Kajiki city was destroyed by fire.

My mother says, "How did we spend the days after the raid? I don't remember. We were completely lost."

After WW2

On August 15, just a few days after the raid, there came the Emperor's announcement of the end of the war – what is called the Imperial Rescript on the Termination of the Greater East Asia War. People were on the devastated land. Sadako just felt relieved as she knew there would be no air raid.

"The next day after the announcement, the sky looked so clear and bright. I saw a plane flying over me, but I knew it would not shoot us anymore. That was a huge comfort."

She remembers no one was crying for the loss of the war. They just had to go on living. There is no photo from this period.

For anyone, life after the war was unpredictable. For Sadako, living with Tsuma alone was tough. Tsuma had an eccentric side that anyone would notice. All her relatives called her a strange, impulsive person. There were numerous times Tsuma lost her temper for unknown reasons and scolded Sadako.

"It always happened out of the blue. When her anger subsided, she asked me to forgive her temper."

She never says what exactly happened.

I, as her grandchild, knew that Tsuma had a temper she struggled to control, and I feared what would happen if she exploded.

"She had magma in her," I say.

"Magma, yes, that was what she had," she nods.

"And she lost Kanesuke unexpectedly early. For her, raising a child alone must have been a challenge."

"I wonder if she really loved me," she says while looking out towards the garden.

"Mum, I'm sure she loved you. She was not a person to care for someone if her heart wasn't there. And she was so proud of you. I remember her telling me how well you did at school."

She grins.

"You know. I was good at behaving like a good student."

"I know, you have a talent."

And I know she couldn't afford to rebel. We both laugh and I am relieved she laughs about it.

At school, Sadako was a cheerful, active student and attracted everyone's attention as a gymnast. She seemed to have had a good life despite there being no man in the family to earn money. Just after the war, there were no jobs available for a middle-aged woman like Tsuma.

Sadako at junior high school

I look at a photo of Sadako and her school friends on stage wearing fairy-like costumes.

"This is from a presentation of creative dance in junior high school," she says.

"It's pretty. Did you start ballet then?"

"Yes, there was no ballet school in Kajiki, so I went to Kagoshima-city on the train every week."

In another photo, she is dancing solo.

"Mum, what I hear from you, I mean your life after the war sounds very different from what I have read in books. Many children nearly starved and widows had to do manual labour."

"You know life in the countryside somewhere like Kajiki is not costly."

"Yes, but I remember Dad told me Sayo had to do road works after the war to support the family. Tsuma didn't work but managed to pay for your ballet lessons. They were so different."

My mother looks thoughtful for a while.

"I have never thought of that."

I again take the oldest album and look for the photo of young Tsuma in Taipei. She is sitting on a bench under a tree in the grounds of the Bank of Taiwan.

"Tsuma was very proud of her career in the bank and loved the life in Taipei. She met Kanesuke there. They lived well until the outbreak of the war. He was a well-known journalist then. They might have earned money in Taiwan."

"Mum, she could even send you to university in Tokyo."

After a pause, she says, "You are right, my university and living costs in Tokyo, they were all from her."

She pours tea for me and asks if I want something sweet. She knows I don't have a sweet tooth but always asks me before she takes some. She puts a small chocolate in her mouth and tastes it slowly.

"Sometimes, a bank clerk from Osaka visited Tsuma with a box of sweets. I watched the beautifully packed Japanese cakes. I remember it as it looked so sophisticated. We never found anything like that in Kajiki."

I break into laughter.

"Here you are, Tsuma must have had an account with a good credit balance."

"She was a mystery, really. How did she live before I knew her? I am so curious," she says.

I remember Tsuma always in plain clothes and imagine her life after the war saving money to raise my mother alone.

Sadako applied for university in Tokyo and was accepted by Kyoritsu women's university. At that time, it was rare to send a daughter to university in Tokyo.

There is a photo of Tsuma standing at Kagoshima station to farewell Sadako. Tsuma is in her best Kimono, Oshima tumugi, (4) looking proud.

University

My mother becomes lively when it comes to talking about her time at university. For her, studying at a university in Tokyo has an essential meaning – a life away from Tsuma, freedom, for the first time.

There is an album from that time, photos of young women and men in Tokyo where the post-war revival energy was overflowing. Kyoritsu women's university was in central Tokyo. Sadako was opening her eyes to the bigger world.

"Tokyo was so far away from Kagoshima, like a foreign city. For Tsuma, it must have been like sending a daughter abroad."

With her classmates, she made friends with architecture students at Waseda University in Tokyo. There is a photo of an open car they rented for a day trip. The group of three boys and three girls are having a picnic in the highlands. Sadako and her two friends wear small collar blouses and flared skirts reaching just below the knee, inspired by the New Look. With the boys, they sit together in a field waving to the camera. In another photo, they are sunbathing in swimming costumes at the seashore. They are smiling with massive hope for their future. People were eager to recover from the war. Social values were changing. Young people accepted ideas such as freedom, equality and individualism in a society where feudalism and totalitarianism were retreating.

In Tokyo, Sadako visited Sayo, the elder sister of Tsuma. Sayo had left Kagoshima and bought a house in Mitaka, a suburb town to live with her two sons. Her younger son Hiroshi had just started to work in an advertising company as one of the first generations of copywriters. For Sadako, it was like meeting him for the first time.

Before graduation, one of the Waseda University students proposed to Sadako. She liked him very much, but after consideration, turned him down. At that time, she was getting to know Hiroshi, my father, and above all, she was concerned about Tsuma.

"I knew he really loved me, but I couldn't accept him. He was from a very good family. Then I considered Tsuma." She pauses and looks away towards the garden. "In those days, it was normal to take care of parents. Tsuma was certain to live with me. And you know, she had an eccentric character."

For Tsuma, Hiroshi, the son of her sister, was no stranger.

"Is Tsuma the reason you married dad?" I ask with hesitation.

"No, I really liked your dad's placid personality. The time with my boyfriend was like a dream. I couldn't plan my life with him."

I look at her. She is flipping through the pages of the album. She starts to talk about my father.

"My university was near his office. He said there were many part-time jobs for students at his work, so I went with my friends. That was how it started."

They became closer after he asked her to model for the advertising campaign for miso soup.

In the willow box, there is the commercial photo for the miso brand. There is my mother, smiling with a bowl of miso soup, looking like a young wife. An idealized image of a family where a wife is caring for her husband.

After the photoshoot, he took her to a plain yakitori counter. It was very different from the trendy restaurant where her university boyfriend took her.

"Somehow, I felt safe with your dad," she says.

Many photos follow after the miso advertisement. Among them, my eyes are drawn to the photograph of my mother on an escalator in a grand department store. She is looking back at the camera, smiling.

"Is it another commercial photo with a cameraman?"

"No, your dad took it."

"Really? Not bad at all."

In the photo, she is looking towards my father with complete trust. They were in love. It didn't take long before my father decided to marry her. Sadako was twenty-three and Hiroshi was thirty-three.

Hiroshi and Sadako just before the marriage

With Grandmothers

I then pick up another album made with a deep navy-blue fabric. It is printed on the cover with 'Album' in gilt characters. It is the wedding album of my parents from 1957. In the wedding photo, my mother is in a simple knee-length taffeta dress with my father in a black tuxedo. After the formal portrait of the couple, there are many casual shots of her. She is talking to her friends, laughing, and smiling at the guests. Her face is radiant, my father looks gentle and everyone is celebrating.

Their married life started with Tsuma in Tanashi, a small city in the western part of Tokyo. Before the marriage, Tsuma had sold the house in Kajiki and moved there. After a year, my mother fell pregnant and left her job at a publishing company. It was the custom for a woman to give up work when she had a child.

At my birth, Tsuma was very excited, as my birthday is the same as Kanesuke's death day. She said I was a reincarnation of him.

There are photos from that time. Three of us, my mother, Tsuma and me sitting together with toys around us. In the monochrome photo, our faces stand out against the dark background. In the dimly lit room with tatami mats divided by sliding doors, Tsuma holds me and looks content.

Sadako, Kumi and Tsuma

Before I turned two years old, my uncle was transferred to Osaka for his job. He asked my father to live with their mother Sayo in Mitaka, while he was away. My father didn't refuse as it was normal for a son to take care of his mother. Tsuma minded greatly as it meant she would be left alone. Mitaka was only six kilometres away, but Tsuma hardly visited us while we were there.

In Mitaka, my mother felt oppressed by Sayo who had no qualms about controlling everything in the house. She had the temperament of the old Japanese family norms and believed it was natural to obey elders. At home, men were more important and so were the elder women. She insisted that my father had a bath first. However late he came home, she made my mother wait for him. Often my mother had to take me to a public bath before I fell asleep. I can't recall my father being at home very much. In the

1960s, he was a promising copywriter. For him, working was a lot more stimulating than being a husband and father.

The only time I remember with my father was when he took me along to pick up my mother and my newly born baby sister from the hospital. I was excited to meet her, but in the taxi, neither of my parents spoke a word. Back at home, my mother had to do all the housework while taking care of a newborn.

After three years, my uncle's family came back. We were meant to go back to Tanashi, but Tsuma refused and raged against Sayo, saying she was selfish. She even told my mother to build a house in a part of Sayo's premises and live there. This situation went on for many months. During that time, two families, nine of us lived under one roof.

Sayo seemed to seize her two daughters-in-law, determined to keep everything in line with her will. My mother and my aunt were totally obedient to her. Sayo was fastidious and wanted the house spotless all the time. Although we children hardly had any direct interactions with Sayo, we were always holding our breath at home. She didn't like us to move around and make any big noise at home. My two cousins and I were always told to play outside. I don't think we enjoyed this time as Mitaka had already been developed as a residential area and there was no open space for us to play in. We just wandered around paved streets.

Very rarely, we were given the freedom to buy things at a local candy shop. I remember the day we went there and spent a long time deciding what to buy. I finally made my mind to buy small rice crackers and a deep blue toy ring. Once we were back home, my aunt told us to show Sayo what we had bought. We went to Sayo's room which was directly connected to the main dining room. My cousins showed the items to her before I did and quickly went back to their room. I was left alone with Sayo.

"We were given money today and went to the shop and I bought these." I showed her what I had bought.

She looked at the deep blue ring and said, "It is a noble colour."

I was surprised as I never had expected any positive words from her.

I asked her, "Do you like the colour?"

"It is an elegant colour," she said.

I knew she really meant it.

Then I asked her, "Would you like to eat some rice crackers? I bought a lot."

"No, I am not hungry," she said unequivocally as always.

After a moment of silence, I said to her again, "Grandma, why don't you keep one. You can eat it when you feel hungry."

She looked at me and took one. It was the only personal conversation with her I remember from our time in Mitaka.

The life of two families living in a small house continued until the day I had a high fever of unknown cause. I was separated from my cousins and slept alone in a tatami-mat room next to the dining room. The doctor told my mother there might be severe health consequences. She called Tsuma that night. Tsuma came at once and stayed beside me.

When I opened my eyes the next morning, what I saw was the prominent face of Tsuma as she was leaning over me, so near to my face. She screamed, "Kumi opened her eyes!" several times. Soon my uncle, aunt and my mother came into the room, but not my father. He wasn't at home.

My recovery made Tsuma accept our return to Tanashi. On the day we came back, Tsuma held me and tossed me into the air calling "You are back!" repeatedly.

Although my mother was released from Sayo, she didn't look any happier in Tanashi. My father became more occupied with his work. The 1960s marked a sharp increase in the Japanese economy and the market was expanding. Society was filled with energy and determination to rise from the predicament of the defeat of the war and create a new, richer society. Men worked hard and got together over a drink after work. My father was not an exception. There were days he didn't come home or even if he did, it was after midnight. My mother was left at home.

However, for me, Tanashi was a more pleasant place. There were still thickets and forests and I never got bored with nature. Tsuma wasn't dominant and she preferred to live at her own pace. The only thing we needed to know was that we should not interfere with her. In the house, there was a wall separating our space from hers. She had a smaller but nicer part of the house facing the garden. When we had to talk with her, we went out and walked along the side of the house to the garden. This distance was comfortable after living with Sayo always in the centre of the house.

My mother's reserved manner to Tsuma seemed strange considering their relationship of parent and child. She always seemed to be on edge, and I got used to her mood. Sometimes, when I came home from school to find my mother wasn't there, I felt relieved. On such a day, I would throw down my school bag and go exploring in the nearby woods or bring my friends to Tsuma's garden. Tsuma was never a talkative person, and I felt tense when I tried to keep up a conversation with her. Yet, she picked a persimmon off the tree in the garden and peeled it for us.

Tsuma died from a cerebral haemorrhage when I was ten. Since it was so sudden, I couldn't even weep. The funeral was carried out in the Shinto style at home. My mother looked emotionless, and no one was crying. I felt deeply guilty about her death as it was caused by an accident at my school when she brought me an umbrella. She fell down outside the classroom and hit the back of her head hard. Before they closed the coffin, I went to my room alone to my bookshelf. Someone followed me. I thought it was my mother, but what I heard behind me was my father's voice. He asked me what I was doing. I replied to him with my back turned to him that I was looking for the book 'grandma' enjoyed the most. I always talked about books to her and let her read some which I enjoyed. She wasn't a book person, and I knew she tried very hard to catch up with me. She always told me what she thought of a book I recommended to her. Nobody else knew that. I put 'A Dog of Flanders' in her coffin.

During the funeral, I observed the almost indifferent attitude of my mother with a little resistance.

A distance

Soon after Tsuma's death, my parents decided to renovate the house. They made a large living room connected with an open kitchen facing the garden. My father bought a stereo set to install in the living room. The choice of everything else was left to my mother. She became engaged and we came to see her creative side. She started by making intricate artificial flowers, then shifted to making dolls before settling down to dressmaking. I was confused by the sudden change in her despite no discernible difference in my father's behaviour. He continued his usual way of life, working late, drinking with his friends, coming home well after midnight. My little sister and I were used to his absence. Christmas and birthdays without him were typical. My mother seemed to endure it all and tried to make those special days as lovely as possible. She shopped at the sales and brought amusing gifts within a limited budget. It was only Sunday afternoon when we saw my father. He woke up late and ate the lunch she cooked for him alone. He was always sullen at home.

In such a life, a postcard came to my mother. I picked it up from the mailbox and handed it to her. She put it on the small table in the living room. For days, it was there. One afternoon, I asked her, "What is that postcard?"

She picked it up and said, "It is an invitation to the reunion of my junior high school in Kagoshima. It makes me feel nostalgic."

"Oh, when is it?"

"Next month, in June."

"Why don't you go? You can meet your friends again. I can take care of things while you are away."

"I wish I could go. But it is expensive to go there, the railway cost is high."

"Why don't you ask Dad?"

I looked at my mother who was holding the postcard tightly.

The next morning, I heard the sound of the closing door when my father was leaving to go to work. I quickly changed from my pyjamas into a one-piece and quietly went out to catch up with him. I ran and called him at the little bridge spanning the small river before the station.

He turned back to me and said, "What?"

"Mum is invited to the reunion in Kagoshima next month. She really wants to go. Could you please tell her to go?"

I tried to keep a smile on my face while talking to him.

He looked at me for some seconds and said, "I see."

Then he turned to the other side and walked towards the station.

Nothing seemed to happen afterwards.

Every night my father came home drunk and often in a taxi with his friends who had also missed the last train. My mother prepared futons for them, woke them up in the morning, and gave them breakfast before they left for work with my father. She never complained, not once. I shared the same breakfast table with them. My father looked more connected with them than us.

In early June, I asked my mother if she would go to the reunion. She replied, "No."

On the surface, my mother seemed to do her daily chores calmly, but twice, she went away without warning. The first time was just after Tsuma's death. She phoned home from somewhere in the late afternoon and said she would come home the next day. Her voice was surprisingly soft, a gentle tone that I had never heard at home. I cooked some instant noodles and ate them with my sister, watched TV longer than usual. After I made her go to bed, I waited until after midnight for my father. He was drunk but surprised to see me opening the door. I told him my mother would return the next day. He said, "Is that so?" and nothing else. I woke him up the following day. He left home for work quickly. The breakfast I managed to make was a bowl of steamed rice and seasoned seaweed. My sister didn't complain about its plainness. We went to school as usual with friends.

156

When I came back from school, my mother was vacuuming in the living room.

The second time was sometime later, in the same year of the reunion invitation. It was Saturday and there was no afternoon class. When I came home, there was a note addressed to me on the dining table. Three times, I read it; my mother would go to refresh herself. I placed the note on the table. In it, she asked me to take care of my sister while she was away. I had no idea where she went but somehow, I knew she would come back soon. I told my sister that she was travelling and again waited for my father until midnight. On Sunday, he was at home looking sour. He told me several times to make tea. He had no idea how to make tea himself. He sat quietly in the living room reading his books. Well after one in the afternoon, he said we would go out to eat something. We walked to the other side of the station where casual restaurants were plentiful. He entered a Chinese noodle shop and we followed him. It was busy, but we managed to sit at a round table. My sister and I didn't understand anything on the menu other than ordinary noodles, so we had ramen. We ate very quietly and walked straight back home. Later in the evening after seven, again he said we would go out and took us to the same place. This time, there were many empty tables, but he sat at the same table as we did for lunch. Then he ordered the same noodles for us while briefly asking, "Are you okay with the same dish?" The food was served, and I stared at the noodles which were precisely the same in appearance as those I had eaten hours ago. I was stunned but didn't want my little sister to notice my upset. We were so used to my mother's cooking that changed every day. I shifted my eyes to the interior of the restaurant. The wall was covered with white synthetic wallpaper that reflected the fluorescent light sharply. It was deserted and almost tranquil except for occasional sounds from the kitchen. I watched my father's expressionless face while eating my noodles but never looked him in the eye. The cook was staring at us across the counter and it made me feel more uncomfortable. We didn't eat up and my father said we would go. My sister stuck with me all day and we hardly conversed with my father.

The next day, when I came home from school, my mother was in the kitchen, looking as if she had just been shopping. She cooked supper as usual and my sister and I ate with huge comfort. Life continued without any change.

We never asked her where she had been after either of her absences.

Parties

In the willow box, there are photos of my parents laughing with my father's friends in the living room. Despite the awkward mood in the family, my father started to invite his friends for the weekend. Around that time, he became chief director of the creative department in his company. In the seventies, it was common for a superior to invite his juniors to his house. However, he was a little different. He asked people from various professions, and it seemed like there was a rule that they didn't talk about business. He wanted to know about them. There, people talked freely, drank a lot and thanked my mother for her hospitality when they left. At first, I felt like I was watching a stage play. He looked like a good father who invites his friends to our home. But backstage, it was my mother who prepared everything to make the day pleasurable. I tried to keep a distance from these regular parties, but soon knew it was impossible. The house wasn't big enough for me to hide all day. The guests came in the early afternoon and stayed until very late. I had to eat dinner with them. Gradually I became involved in these events – my mother asked me to help with the shopping she needed to do for the parties. She took me to Tsukiji market for fish and Ameyoko Arcade for imported ingredients.

Around that time, my father started sea fishing and soon, decided to treat his friends to the fish he caught. My mother increasingly refined her cooking skills and made almost professional-standard sushi. One Saturday, he came home proudly with a large black sea bream. Naturally, at the next day's party, the main dish was sushi, his catch of the day. She made beautiful sushi each carefully wrapped with a shiny bamboo leaf.

When my father said, "It is sushi, made with the sea bream I caught yesterday," everybody raised their voices in surprise. He let me taste one. The combination of the whitefish, rice lightly seasoned with vinegar and the scent of a bamboo leaf: I had never tasted anything so delicate. I looked at my mother who was watching the reaction to her sushi. They savoured sushi quietly for a while and said it was the best sushi they had ever had. She smiled and said from the other side of the kitchen counter, "There is more if you like." She looked alive.

It was not only eating and drinking. My father and his friends listened to music together. Despite it being late at night, he played records of various symphonies at a loud volume. My mother asked me to turn the volume down but as soon as I did, he put it up high again and said, "From here, it is going to be the climax."

As my father spent his puberty in the totalitarian regime of wartime, it seemed he was making up for a lost time, indulging his passion for literature, visual arts and music that had been forbidden in his youth. He enjoyed talking about these topics with his friends, as if he was trying to recapture the springtime of his life. My mother, who was ten years younger than him, was a realist and welcomed the gradual change in her husband.

Frequent parties made our living room a casual salon with writers, musicians, professors, photographers and master artisans of Buddhist imagery. They were all unique characters and spoke to me as a person, not as a child. I appreciated this and often stayed with them, listening to their conversations.

After every party, my mother cleaned the room, did the dishes and never looked fed up. I joined her after midnight when my father had gone to bed upstairs. When we finished, it was often nearly 3 a.m.

Real or not

In other albums in the willow box, there are no grandmothers. Six years after Tsuma's death, Sayo died of cancer. At her death, all family members gathered at her bed in Mitaka. She was conscious until her last moment.

A few weeks after the funeral, my mother called me from downstairs. When I came down to the living room, she was sitting on the floor formally, not on a chair. I sat across from her. There were two cups of green tea already on the table.

"I think I can tell you now as you are old enough."

I looked at her tense face.

"Tsuma is not your grandmother. I was an adopted child."

She looked at my face, worried as if she expected me to be upset. I quietly said, "I knew it."

"What?"

The first summer holiday after Tsuma's death, I was eleven, staying with my father's relative in Kagoshima. That evening, after supper, they started to talk about my parents. Since I had never heard about their childhoods, I asked the old lady in the family.

"Did they know each other when they were living here?"

She replied, "Oh, I don't think so. Hiroshi was about to go to Navy school when Sadako was adopted and came here."

Her daughter anxiously stopped her.

"Hasn't Sadako told you?" she asked me apologetically.

For the first time, I realized there was no resemblance between them. My mother is small and has a soft, roundish face, whereas my grandmother was tall, broad and had a long face. The subtle distance my mother kept from her had a reason. The conversation became awkward. Soon they told me to go to bed.

In bed, I listened to the chorus of frogs outside while numerous little things about my grandmother appeared in my mind. I smiled at her.

Next morning, they asked me if I had slept well. I replied, "Yes," and was off to swimming.

Now, facing my mother who looked totally confused, I explained to her briefly how I had known about it.

"How horrible of them to tell you so carelessly!" She said furiously.

"Mum, she thought you had already told me. I felt sorry as she was so shocked to see my reaction. She didn't mean badly."

She said slowly,

"Tsuma really loved you and didn't want you to know she was not a real grandmother."

What is real and not real? That is something I have been thinking about since then.

"Mum, if you say a blood relation, I have a distant link with her. She is a sister of Dad's mother, right?"

"…yes."

She was losing words.

"Mum, don't worry, her not being a REAL grandmother, it doesn't matter to me."

I ran up to my room and sobbed a little. I didn't understand why she had to wait so long to tell me. For me, Tsuma and Sayo were my grand-mothers. The existence of her biological mother didn't cross my mind. She might have started to talk about her real family if I hadn't broken our conversation.

A loss

In high school, I began to view myself and everything around me critically. I felt I was like an automatic train running on a fixed rail. Like many in puberty, I felt suffocated by my surroundings. Books seemed to be the only way I could expand my mind and the English language we studied at school was the window that opened up a different world. Instead of going to university in Japan as many of my friends opted to do, I told my parents that I wanted to study abroad. They were puzzled. My father said none of his acquaintances had ever studied abroad. My mother looked confused and started to treat me gingerly. When we were alone at home, she said in a very gentle voice,

"You don't need to worry so much. You can go to university here. And, you will find a nice person to marry."

That instantly touched a nerve.

"That is not the point, mum!"

How much I didn't want to fall into a life of a housewife like her, was something I couldn't dare to say. I stopped talking with her for a while.

Around that time, something terrible happened. My uncle became ill. After numerous examinations, he was diagnosed with brain cancer. This terrible news shocked all of us but especially my father. For him, my uncle was much more than a brother. Since their parents separated before the war, my uncle had supported the family. Even after my parents' marriage, he was the mainstay holding all the family together.

My father spent a lot of his time with my uncle and even started to talk more with us about his illness. My mother spent most of her days at the hospital, to help my aunt care for my uncle. We were slowly connecting together. Everyone was praying for his recovery. However, cancer took him away from us fast. He was fifty-seven.

At the funeral, I saw my father staring vacantly into space. It didn't feel real to me either. Our family without his existence was unimaginable. I felt very sorry for my cousins but couldn't say anything to them. After the funeral, my father constantly visited Mitaka and helped my aunt to clean the house and the garden.

At home, we saw a dramatic change in him. He now came back early from work and ate with us. Sometimes, we met near his office after his work, walked through a department store together, and had dinner at a restaurant. At work, he agreed to act as a go-between for his juniors. It meant the involvement of my mother as they would attend as a couple to assist a bride and groom. She only complained lightly when it became too frequent an occurrence. She looked busy and happy.

One day, at supper, my father told me I could go abroad to study but on one condition.

"I knew you would go to university anyway. I was ready to support you if you decide to study outside Tokyo, for example, in Kyoto." He meant he would help me financially for four years with the estimated cost of Japanese university fees and the living costs.

"If you can study abroad within this budget, you can go wherever you decide."

I learned later my father's decision came from his conversation with my uncle at the hospital – when my uncle asked about me, my father told him about my intention. My uncle supported me and told my father to let me go if I was really serious. My mother went along with my father's decision. I sent an application form to London.

In April 1978, I went to Haneda airport with my parents. Before checking in, I conversed with my high school friends who came to see me off. I was so tense and hardly talked to my parents. They merely said, "Take care." I looked at them from a distance when I was leaving the check-in counter. They were standing tightly together, looking worried. I waved to them a few times and turned around to the gate.

Later my mother told me that when the plane took off, she burst into tears. When they returned home from the airport, the cherry blossoms were in full bloom in the garden.

A widow and grandmother

While I was away, I wrote to my parents respectively. The distance and the time gap helped me to see them as individuals. Especially with my father, the way we communicated by letters brought us a better understanding of each other. And I got to know the change in their lives. Before he reached the official retirement age, my father couldn't retain his job as an executive in his company. The salary he received for his new job fell by almost half, and my mother got a part-time job in a relative's company. Life totally dependent on my father's salary was over. She commuted in the rush hour, worked with people at a ceramic wholesaler.

My father came to see her differently. They occasionally ate out after work and went to concerts together. At the weekend, they shared a small house with other people at the seaside in Miura peninsula. It was almost a two-hour train journey from home. They took a train on Saturday morning, stayed one night and came back on Sunday evening. My mother recalls this time as the most peaceful they had spent together.

"It was so quiet there, we sat together at the seashore after nightfall. In the darkness, we saw two little shining eyes approaching us. We knew him. The black cat of the neighbouring house. He came every time we were there."

When I returned after four years studying in London, my parents looked more together than ever.

After working for three years in Tokyo, I met my husband, Nobu. My decision to marry came as a big surprise to my parents. My father told his friends I had an air that I wasn't interested in such a conventional relation as marriage. He was right. I myself felt odd about my decision, but I was comfortable with Nobu's open-mindedness and liked his sense of humour. And there was one thing I had told him before we got married. I said I never wanted to be a wife in the traditional way. He looked at me as if I had said something completely bizarre and asked me playfully, "Which era are we living in?" We both laughed.

In my wedding album from 1985, there are photos of twenty-five-year-old me in a white one-piece my mother found in a boutique. She knew I wouldn't wear any of the rental decorative long dresses included in the wedding ceremony fee and was eager to find a dress without any ornament. I liked the midi-length dress with its delicate flare from top to bottom. Then, I was so full of myself that I didn't even realize how much she cared for me.

After the marriage, my father often invited us and his friends for the weekend. My mother cooked, and I cleared the table as in the past. She looked happy to see my father and Nobu together.

She says now, "He really enjoyed the time with Nobu. It was as if he knew there wasn't much time left for him."

One very early morning at the beginning of September 1987, we had a call from my sister. "Dad collapsed." She was almost sobbing at the other end of the line. When my husband and I arrived at the emergency department, I saw my mother and my sister standing in the corridor helplessly. Soon the doctor came out of the room and said he was very sorry. He told us it was a myocardial infarction. My mother screamed weakly and repeated, "It can't be true." And my sister continued to touch my father's dead body that was still warm, like a small child. I could not walk to the stretcher where my father was laid. I stood stiff with my husband just a few meters away but felt everything far more distant. My mother asked me in a faint voice, "Please call his friends."

Despite such a sudden death, many people came to the wake and the funeral which took place at home. My mother was too upset to organize things as a chief mourner. It was my father's friend who arranged the funeral and the events that came after. People who had come to the parties in the past, and the colleagues my father used to work with came voluntarily to help us.

In the kitchen, I saw two young women washing up used cups. I had never met them. I said, "Thank you very much for your help, but how did you find your way here?" One of them smiled and showed me a small piece of paper saying, "Our boss gave us this map."

It was a copy of my father's hand-written map showing the way to our house from the station. The house was marked with a square with 'MY HOUSE'. I stared at his firm handwriting.

I asked her, "Could I have this please?" She said, "Of course," and gently handed it to me.

"It is amazing someone kept it for so long," I said.

"My boss told me it's from the time of the parties."

I smiled at her and said, "My father really enjoyed them."

For almost a year after his death, my mother was very moody and unsettled. She called me in the evening to come to eat with her and asked me to stay while she was taking a bath. She said she thought my father would live with her forever. Death at sixty-one was early, and she was at fifty-one a widow.

Gradually, she started to show signs of recovery. She decided to see her friends from university, visited relatives and school friends in Kagoshima, joined a local Tai-chi class and unexpectedly became a grandmother. She was excited about the arrival of my first son. I never saw her so openly happy with a person. And after four years, my second son was born.

Sadako with her first grandson

Now, we move from the albums to unmounted individual photos in the willow box. It is impossible to sort them out. Instead, we take one out randomly and talk about it. I pick up a photo of my mother laughing with my sons in her kitchen. Being a good cook, she always fed them with

164

her homemade food. I can see my sons asking her what's for lunch. In a Christmas photo with my sons, she is all smiles, such a smile as I never saw in my childhood.

She talks beside me, "I am very fortunate to have such happy times with my grandchildren."

"Mum, are grandchildren very different from children?"

She pauses for a while and says, "How should I put it, it is like I am free from day-to-day responsibility for them and just can cherish them," and continues, "You've done well. I can't imagine how to raise such energetic boys. I had only girls."

"Raising boys is physically exhausting, but girls can't be easy."

She glances at me and says, "Oh, my parenting, if it can be called so, was such a mess. It feels like you grew up alone while many things were happening," she laughs lightly and after a long pause says, "you were not an easy child."

I see her gentle eyes and say for the first time, "You always looked stressed at home."

My mother looks at me for a while and says, "I felt my world had suddenly shrunk after marriage."

"It must have been such a drastic change. Mum, when I was small, I thought being a housewife was horrible."

"I can understand. Your grandmothers were both difficult to live with."

My mother stops talking. She stands up and moves to the veranda to take in the dry laundry. I join her. The wind blows calmly outside. From the veranda, I look down at the garden which used to be Tsuma's territory. There she had chickens to lay eggs and did washing at the well. She cooked fish over a charcoal fire and hardly used the kitchenette inside. She carried on living an almost rural lifestyle in Tokyo. It was the same for Sayo, but unlike Tsuma who did everything by herself, Sayo forced people to follow her orders. My mother once told me that, in the early 1950s, after moving to Tokyo, Sayo refused to use gas in the kitchen and insisted on using an earthen charcoal brazier in the garden. Even years later, she made my mother wash dishes at the well in winter.

My mother says, "It must sound crazy for you but then, for Sayo, it was unimaginable to pay money for fire and water."

Sayo and Tsuma led simple lives, they hardly bought anything for themselves. But outside, everything was changing. How did they see the newly westernized lifestyles and industrial society where people strived to produce and consume? There was a massive gap between their old values and what was happening around them.

I say, "Mum, were they really such difficult women? They might not be so different from other people in their generation."

She turns to me and looks as if she is waiting for me to say more.

"After the war, wasn't it so confusing for them moving from Kagoshima to Tokyo to live a new phase of life? I know you had a hard time with Sayo and Tsuma, but weren't they having a hard time too?"

She says, "Yes, the change in life after the war was crazy. The prewar values turned over."

"It could be just that they tried hard not to lose themselves."

She nods to me. Her expression is much more relaxed now.

"Your aunt and I can now laugh about the hard times we had with Sayo. We wonder why we were so submissive to her."

"Oh, what do you think?"

"I think I was a coward. I didn't want any trouble. It might have been better for Sayo if we had argued. She would have been offended for sure, but it could have formed a different kind of relationship between us," and she continues, "it could have caused a huge fuss, but at least we would have been livelier and your dad might have liked it better."

I listen to her.

Visits

On TV, the prime minister is announcing he will improve the supply of face masks available on the market. He never says when. They have been out of stock for more than a month. The empty shelf in a drug store has a written notice: "*Dear customers, please take only one packet.*" People are anxious about these shortages. A face mask has become a symbol of protection.

When I phoned her to visit again to see the photos, she mentioned a TV program on handmade masks.

"It is effortless. You only need a large handkerchief and a pair of rubber bands."

From Tanashi station, I stroll a little rather than directly going to her house. I keep watching the ground on both sides of the street. There, little wild violets silently gather in crevices. It is the same purple violet I used to find in the forest not far from home, now a golf practice range. The land development hasn't obliterated their habitat. They are resilient. I look around to find more, just like I did as a child. There are a few more at the edge of the garden of a nearby house. I take off my face mask, crouch down and look at the discreet existences for a while. It is spring.

"Did you find out how to make a handkerchief mask?" she asks me in her living room.

"Yes, thanks. I made one already at home. It was so easy."

She looks satisfied.

I say to her, "Mum, could I see your real family's photos again?"

"Of course, do you want to go upstairs now?"

We go and open the oldest album. I look carefully. Apart from the photo of her biological parents, there is only a small, very faded photo of her grandmother sitting on a chair alone.

She says, "We must have taken more before my mother's death. But I don't have them."

"Please don't worry. I just was curious about your brother."

I remember the afternoon he visited her. I happened to be at home after the mid-term exams. From the morning, she looked excited. She told me a male friend she knew at university time was coming. When the doorbell rang, we saw him holding a big potted orchid. He was uplifted with joy, his face was almost red. "Welcome," she said in a shrill voice and they didn't speak for a while looking at each other. I felt something special between them and thought that he was her brother. After a brief greeting, I left them alone in the living room and went to my room.

"My brother said he had worked very hard with the hope of seeing me when he became successful."

"So, that was the day he had been longing for."

"Yes. He had a tough life. During the time of food shortage, he wasn't fed well. And he was very lonely. After the war, he stormed out of the house when he was still a teenager." She talks continuously about what he had told her on that day.

When she stops talking, I volunteer to make English tea. It is getting cold upstairs.

"Mum, shall I bring the tea up here?"

"Yes, please." My mother always says I make better tea than anybody else in the family.

I bring milk tea and place the tray on the floor. She tastes it and says it is very, very, good. Slowly, tea warms us up. She looks relaxed.

"Have you kept contact with him since then?" I ask.

"He invited us once to Yamanashi while you were in England. We met his wife and two daughters and spent two days together but after that, I lost contact with him. His business went bankrupt."

I don't know what to say.

"Oh, that's sad."

"Yes, it is sad. And I heard recently he had passed away."

I look at her.

"It must be a shock for you."

"There are things we can't help."

She stops talking. The thought comes to my mind that her father would have been gone long ago. We sip tea quietly.

After a long silence, she says, "I went to see my father just after the death of Tsuma."

That took me by surprise as I never thought of that.

"Did you have the contact address?"

"No, but Tsuma kept it. I found the address and just took the train."

"You went back to the house you were born in?"

"No, Kofu city was bombed badly during the war. They had moved to a different house after the war."

I hold the teacup with both hands.

"Once in the town, I could find the house easily. It was a traditional Japanese house. There wasn't a doorbell, so I slid the entrance door open and called inside. 'Excuse me. Is anyone there?' An old woman in kimono came out. That was his wife. She asked me politely, 'May I ask your name?' and all of a sudden, from the far end of the corridor, there was the voice of a man. 'Is it Sadako?' I replied, 'Yes, it is me.' It was my father who called my name."

I take a breath. I can only say, "That is amazing."

Her eyes are filled with tears.

"Maybe my voice sounded like my mother's. He said he had thought I would come someday."

His wife welcomed my mother, and they persuaded her to stay one night. It must have been the day she phoned from somewhere and told me she would come home the next day.

"Could you talk with your father?"

"Yes, but not really. Men are useless, aren't they? He was hesitant for fear of annoying his wife. I was hoping to hear what happened afterwards, how other family members lived, especially about my grandmother as I had stayed with her after my mother's death until I left for Kagoshima. But my father only said, 'I tried to convince myself that I had given a daughter in marriage very young,' and nothing else."

The visit to her father led her to realize we were her only family. My mother stuck with the marriage. Was it because endurance was seen as a condition of being female? Even after WW2 with the wave of westernization, the national mentality didn't change rapidly. It was still hard for women who wished to live differently. But my mother never seemed to have tried to change her life. She had her own understanding of life. Through her life, with her adoption and the war, she knew life could become fragile at any time. Even with the difficulties she faced, she wanted to keep her family. And above all, she seemed to love my father unconditionally.

In the last few years of their married life, my parents had a strong bond, with acceptance and dependence, and there was an empathy between them.

Cherry blossoms

There have been some windy nights. Cherry blossoms are past full bloom, they are scattering. The playground in front of the public library is partially white with petals. We have promised to meet here this afternoon. The library has been closed for weeks. Small children are running around in the playground and their mothers watch them from the benches.

My mother, a large part of her face covered, with a gauze mask, is walking towards me, only her eyes visible. I wave at her.

We each sit on each small individual benches.

"It is so hard to recognize people with face masks. How are you managing, Mum?"

"I am alright. And how are Aki and Ken doing? Are they keeping themselves safe?"

She hasn't seen my sons for some time.

"Yes, they are okay. Everything is online now. They all work from home."

"So, you are busy cooking for them."

"Yes, I am."

"It is good, at least you can all eat together."

"Mum, they are asking about you. Why don't we set up something like Skype? Then, you can see them."

"I want to do that."

"I will help you to set it up."

"Yes, please."

It is strange to talk to each other with face masks on. Not seeing her expression makes me feel awkward.

From nowhere, pigeons gather rapidly near us to pick at something on the ground. The couple sitting a few meters away from us are throwing tiny pieces of bread at them. We watch the movement of the pigeons for a while. The couple stand up and walk towards the station. Pigeons fly away in the blink of an eye.

Then we shift our eyes to the children again. They are calling their mothers who are now standing at the edge of the playground.

"Mothers have nowhere to take their children after the closure of the schools," I say.

"Not only schools. I wonder how they spend their days," my mother says with sympathy.

"It is hard to stay home all day with children. Those children are so lucky to have this playground nearby."

"Very fortunate children. They have mothers to take them here," she says in a deep voice.

Her eyes are shining. She continues, "Look at their faces, they are so carefree."

They are tired of rope skipping and start a ball game.

I say, "Mum, sometimes, I think of future generations, what they are going to face." I continue, "Have we ever expected this? This pandemic," I say carefully.

"No," she says in a clear voice.

"We can't imagine what kind of day it will be tomorrow." I turn around to my mother. She is still looking towards the playground.

"At my age, a day is life. When I go to bed, I thank my body that gave me my day. And in the morning, I am thankful I am alive."

I stare at her calm profile, an eighty-four-year-old woman.

"Mum, it is true. We live only at this moment, just now."

A girl is running toward us, chasing a small ball.

I get up, pick up the ball and throw it gently to her.

She catches it and waves to me.

In the distance, the girl's mother bows to us.

We bow back.

The wind starts blowing again. We look up at the cherry blossoms. Many are on the branches, still. They sway in the wind. So quiet.

Reference

1. Futon: Japanese quilted mattress

2. Udon: Japanese noodle made from flour

3. The Potsdam Declaration: The final declaration of surrender request to Japan on July 26, 1945, in the names of the United Kingdom, The United States, and the Republic of China.

4. Oshima tsumugi: The traditional textile of the Amami archipelago (mainly Amami Oshima) in the south of Kagoshima prefecture. This refers to a silk cloth hand-woven with mud-dyed threads. The abbreviation is "Oshima".

FULL CIRCLE

_____

Vayu Naidu

India & England

Writing rejuvenated the companionship I shared with my mother Jaya. It has brought to light the woman I perhaps took for granted, and now see her in a historical time and indeed in another dimension. There are many agents that shaped her narrative. Common to her generation: World War Two. Specific to her identity: India emerging independent, women's higher education, milk and teeth, the realms of the gods with a firm seat in a perennial philosophy. It has given me a paradigm to live by and not be subsumed solely by western discourse in modern India. That philosophy helps me to integrate my pan-Indian linguistic routes and the cosmic. She made life come full circle.

I started to write this to experience what the transmission of a mother is. I wanted so much to share some of these values for the children of the future, with their mothers. In this sense, Sellars's observation defines self-discovery. For me, it is about tracing my mother's routes to self-affirmation.

* * *

'Every culture on Earth has primary and foundational myths, legend and stories, which understand that in order to find yourself, you have to leave your own country and your own people and go to a distant land where you will be challenged, amazed, and transformed and where, in adversity, you will meet your hidden heroic self and find friends you never imagined you would have. It has long been understood across cultures and across civilizations that none of us are who we appear to be to our immediate family and friends and that it is only in a far-away place that we begin to discover other selves, other possibilities that lie within us.' (2014)

So, this is social document that is personal history combining public fact with an interleaving of myth and poetry. It is the essence of what makes a her-self, and in transmission, made my-self, to pass on to all children. There are two external objects of association that have inspired this. One, a tattered, ruled notebook of History with faded blue ink doodles in English about Imperial economics and a dentist appointment c. 1942. The second, a Sanskrit poem Jaya, my mother, was reading before she died c.2006. She had scribbled notes to certain verses she had sung to me earlier. Each of these objects had a story; these were handed to me by my father as a recognition of our circle of time mapped by three dots that moved in multiplications. The unities of historical time, cosmic time, and the infinity of love.

Mapping Loss Filling Time

'Mamaa! You had me,
But I never had you...'

– John Lennon

November 24, 2007

The date is etched in my memory. It is, as we say in India, when mother 'departed' from her body. The body was cremated on a day of northeast monsoon rain. My father carried his wife's ashes in a terracotta pot and released them in the Bay of Bengal by Chennai. The 'atma', or soul of a person named as Jayarukmini Naidu, 83, was set free. This is a Hindu commemoration of the dead and we do not have gravestones, or a cemetery. So, in the tradition of 'moksha' or release and liberation, nothing brings 'her' back. Except, of course, the memory of an essence of her. I perceived her, crossing between a lifetime of geopolitical maps and historical dates.

1924-2007 and the making of immortality

I think John Lennon's lyrics sum up the huge reservoir of what Mama/ Mother is from the perspective of what can hurt about the 'missing' person – not physically, but the emotional hollow of possibilities it leaves open as an unhealing wound. It made me sit up to what Mother Jaya was, and is to me. The reconciliation is the 'missing', *tanhai* of that companionship; you befriend the loss and the loss becomes the comfort of Mother. Now that she is dead and her ashes absorbed in the sea salt of the coast of the Bay of Bengal, I awaken to small details – among them that we were women who knew what it meant to have a room, at least a view of one's own. She struggled like hell, making life look like heaven for all of us. For a generation when men got on with nation-building and women were feeding mouths and organising extended families, I was fortunate to witness an intellectual and emotional reliance that my father and mother shared.

She gave me a sense of western History with its chronology of linear time. She also gave me the deep imprint of how Indian History accounts for its time cycles through its orality and chronicles by means of mythopoeic history.

An Astrologer had once read her birth chart and said she will die when life is in full swing. When I heard about it, I wanted a date, a time according to my reliable tiny dial of a wristwatch – I could not see the parody of my own asking! What was 'life in full swing'? When was she 'gonna' die?

Just when I relaxed about dates and times and realised that astrology too was a professional livelihood for many, I accelerated my attendance without any significant purpose other than enjoyment, at the celebrations of birthdays, anniversaries, bethrothals, Christmases and Diwalis.

My sister announced my nephew's wedding in Delhi. I was touring a History play about Annie Besant – a figure my mother had introduced to me years ago. Besant is known for the Bryant and May Match Girls Strike in England, and in India for attempting freedom for India through consti-tutional reform. I had commissioned and produced a play for Vayu Naidu Theatre Company funded by Arts Council England. The play was written by Pakistani British playwright Rukhsana Ahmad and the Director was Chris Banfield. It was touring across England, then Allahabad at Annie Besant's stamping ground, Delhi, Chennai. Mum and I would speak on the phone – London – Chennai – every Saturday, and as her birthday was drawing up on December 7, I said we were going to celebrate it a few days later in Chennai, before going on to the wedding in Delhi's winter of 2007.

Cheekily, I had pleaded with Jaya calling from London to her in Chennai, during rehearsals: "Promise me, Mum, you won't fall off to sleep in the play sitting in the front row of Egmore Museum Theatre?" The Theatre is historic for Annie Besant's time in Madras as Chennai was known in the time of establishing the Theosophical Society, where Mum and I had spent time together watching other productions. So this was such an honour to bring a production from England to India with Arts Council England endorsement, Air India, Prakriti Foundation, private sponsorships as well as The University of Allahabad and the Indian Council for Cultural Relations and The High Commission of India.

She laughed. "I'll tell Dad to wake me up when I doze off during the play!" we both laughed.

That night, in London, with four days left to catch the flight with the entire cast, production team and sets, I rolled the gold bangle she gave me for my fiftieth birthday along my wrist and forearm. I was happy in the circumference of what life had given me of my mother and our immortal friendship.

I woke the next morning with thoughts of managing alone, no one to ask to wish me well. I shook myself out of this discombobulation and was walking up to Rehearsal. What a fine golden autumn, air crisp as a

Braeburn apple to the tongue, filling my lungs with life. My mobile buzzed in my jeans, and all Dad on the other end could say was: "She's gone. Mum's gone," his voice folded like a damp tea towel in the winter sun. He collected himself and said, "How much love there is…" My heart cracked into a million of autumn's dry leaves.

That cataclysmic crashing universe of John Lennon's grief was mine. Dad's grief was of knowing her for sixty-two years through three wars, many armed forces service separations, a mind and heart that walked with him from one century of colonialism to a century of India's awakening. It was silently glowing in my mobile in my hand, her heart. Dad later told me the man in charge of the oxygen canister in the hospital where she had been taken had not checked if it was full. My niece Shibani, barely eighteen, has heard mother's soft footsteps in the house at night, after mother died.

When Mother was 82, Chandralekha, the 'Skills' choreographer and dancer of contemporary Bharata Natyam saw my mother. She took me by her hand and with her dazzling, kajal-lined eyes looked at me and said: "Do you even *know* what all your mother has been through and how she contains it all?"

Mother's disability of a growing deafness, possibly with my birth, her fourth, unbearable labour necessitating my caesarean birth in the eighth month, and her constant love, is a mystery to me. If she could not hear, her deep listening was in a uniquely relevant key. This memory is a meditation of the time she walked on the earth, and now that she doesn't, what she has left to the air, and every shimmering leaf from life's speaking tree.

World War Two in pre-Independent India:

She was born in 1924 to Calpakkam Karunanidhi Naidu (CK my grandfather – the first name in south Indian families states the landscape of their origin) and Allarmelu Mangathai (mother's mother). They named my mother Jayarukmini Naidu (seated extreme left – Jaya – victory and Rukmini – god Krishna's wife). Chellamma as she was known (Chellam -home name for 'much loved') was the third child, only daughter/sister to five sons/brothers. She was protective toward even the older two, seated on the right of the photograph, and a 'pack mate' with the younger three, standing. Some of the socio-political landscape that my mother was growing up in is necessary, as Madras is often neglected from commentaries unless it is to do with presidents or judges or temple authorities! The omission of documents about women's education, about non-literate or formally educated mothers in Madras is significant, and I make mention of this to gain a sense of Madras as being different in its ethos from Delhi for the reader to understand the magnitude of migration for a young woman from the south going alone to the north of India during partition around 1947-1948, the time of India's independence.

In the 1910s her father set up South India Exports that included leather and textiles that traded to Germany, Burma and England. Hence, settling in the port of Madras he created a strong Telegu-speaking Naidu community or clan. CK was a philanthropist and interested in the Arts and had an Honours Degree in English Literature from Madras University. He was a co-organiser of the Salt March at the Madras Marina Beach. His friends included the Principal of Presidency College, a Christian, and there were close Muslim friends in the Business community as well as an army of cousins and second cousins who relied on CK's constant caretaking. It was a cosmopolitan, multilingual and diverse company that was homegrown with local languages and customs and had been struck by the emergence of Mohandas Karamchand Gandhi's 'radical' writings and the hope he brought for India breaking free from British colonial rule.

This was in the wake of Annie Besant, also a co-founder of the Theosophical Society in Madras. Allarmellu, CK's wife and Jaya's mother, was a Recitative Telegu poet and held recitation of the epics in their home. She refused to learn 'Butler' English. By this it was understood that if she learned English, she would always be made to feel she was subordinate as it would be functional and in servitude like a Butler; besides she indicated, she had the rich access to local slang, curses, omens and poetic expressions from Telegu her mother-tongue. For her, Telegu, Tamil, Dakhini were the languages of her soul. However, CK, and she knew Chellamma was heading for a new era, sent her to study in an English medium school, Presentation Convent in Vepery, Madras.

1942

India is the jewel in the crown. It is still part of the British Empire and many Indians are fighting for the Allied Forces in Europe, Africa, 'the pacific theatre' Burma. Aban Naidu is a young man who is posted in the Northwest of India in the cause of the Allied forces. Indian lives are read as numbers, an anonymous collective who must sacrifice themselves for the great cause of Greater Britain.

Jayarukmini Naidu, my mother, is eighteen. My mother's education is in English, while her widowed mother's is in Telegu epics. There was a shortage of milk I was told, and that continued to affect my mother's teeth and bones, and she remembered it throughout her initiatives for mothers and children in primary schools where she was Head Teacher. It didn't stop that wide smile that made every dread disappear. The world was connected by the commonwealth of education as power and it was a time of India's awakening, girls dressed in white saris with leg-of-mutton-sleeved blouses supporting the cause for Independence with the milk of human kindness. Not angels, but shaktis – goddesses, summoned on salt marches, indigo riots, cooking, feeding, bandaging, singing, educating, being educated if they could, surviving typhoid, cholera, being given in marriage, bearing the next generation.

Amamma, my mother's mother recited the epics in Telegu, spoke to the servants in Tamil, and the register of Telegu changed depending on the region, caste and proximity of familial relationships of the visitors who arrived at her household in Barnaby Road, Kilpauk, Madras and is lodged in my memory of a three-year-old girl. But the way my grandmother ran her home and household from the age of 29 when her husband CK, my Thata grandfather, died of typhoid. A new pattern was emerging in India's southern political times. My grandmother had five sons and one daughter in a turbulent south that was not prepared, but expecting the invasion from the Japanese via Burma, and surviving unprecedented floods from torrential downpours. Jaya studied in a Presentation convent, learned English, and later continued her MA in History and Economics in Pachai-yappa's College – a Telegu Founder of Education – and the college had been accredited to The University of Madras. Jaya was among the very few of her generation who was 'allowed' education, not out of wealth or necessity, but by inclination and nation-building. Yet, it was considered 'old' if you were beyond your teens and were as yet unmarried.

My father was commissioned on the eighth of November 1942 in the Indian British Army. He was sent to Burma before 1945.

How time flies:
"1946."

The date is written in Quink royal blue fountain pen ink. It's legible. Pure indigo. Mother's Notebook from her History lectures in Pachaiyappa's College, Madras University.

"Japan. World War II. Indians returning. From Rangoon."

2019, on 'WhatsApp' I'm wishing my last living aunt Pramila – my mother's third sister-in-law – a happy birthday. Her daughter, my youngest cousin Lavania is typing my aunt's messages from Pune, Maharashtra where they now live in a gleaming apartment.

(Pramila is Lavania's mother, my aunt. Pramila's father was Dr AD Thiru who was working in the Port Commissioners Office as Administrative Medical officer at Rangoon.

The Japanese raided Burma in 1946...they had a beautiful independent bungalow called 'Rajasthan'.

Then one fine morning it just rained bombs on them.

They left in a hurry, packed a few of their belongings and moved to their friend Mr Bhushanam's home.

My Thatha only picked up amamma's 2 pictures, one bust and a full size with him before leaving their beloved home.

[05:31, 9/11/2019] Lavania: They stayed at the friend's home for 2 days and set sail on the last boat for India called Chilka…arrived in Calcutta after 3 days.

Dr Irawathy … (My Grandmother's cousin) was there to receive them.

The monks from the Ramakrishna Mission were there and served all the passengers hot puri and aloo.

[05:32, 9/11/2019] Lavania: They boarded the train and went to Bangalore where mom's maternal grandfather stayed.

[05:33, 9/11/2019] Lavania: My grandfather did not come as doctors were not allowed to leave the country.

[05:37, 9/11/2019] Lavania: They stayed for a year and then went back to Rangoon.

Visited their old home and to their dismay found that the Japs had ruined it and had used it as a Signals centre.

Could not live there ...the lane was Thompson Avenue.

They moved into Tubantia building on River block.

They stayed here for 3 years till 1950 and then got back to India as Thatha was unwell.

[05:39, 9/11/2019] Lavania: All 3 siblings learnt to play the piano before the war from an Anglo-Indian lady.

My Amama sold her vadyanam (pure twenty-four-carat gold waistband worn as brides) to buy the piano which she did not like.

[05:40, 9/11/2019] Lavania: They all studied in Methodist English Girls high school.

Boys were only till the 4thstd.

[05:42, 9/11/2019] Lavania: Mummy was in the 3rd standard when she left.

She vividly remembers her school and loved the discipline it inculcated.

Her class teacher was Miss Scot...strict but Mummy liked her.

She learnt all her hymns from that school.

[05:45, 9/11/2019] Lavania: However, unfortunately when they returned to Burma they could not continue their studies...so they learnt tailoring and embroidery.

Danny Mama (Pramila's brother) stayed back at Madras to pursue his studies.

[05:46, 9/11/2019] Lavania: Hope this is enough material... Vayuka.

Thanks to you it was nice reviving all old memories.

[05:47, 9/11/2019] Lavania: Mummy wants to know where exactly are you going to use it and how?

We can't talk because Pramila aunty gets emotional about distances and finds it difficult to speak. Besides, the five-and-a-half-hour time difference between me in London and her in Pune makes us feel disembodied. It's the feeling of being buoyed on an ocean of memory that is so tangible, but we are not who we were. She has become the little girl I used to be. Her memory of escaping from Rangoon with her parents, who were doctors, in the last boats to Calcutta grows vivid. The Ramakrishna Mission monks gave them, like many British Indians who returned to India, food and shelter. Pramila was still singing the song her piano teacher had taught her to stop her from trembling. When she met my mother and was to marry my Uncle, Pramila felt she would be comfortable in this new family. My aunt was like my second mother in the extended family.

1946

Jayarukmini married my father, Captain Aban Naidu. For the first anniversary, he bought her Jawaharlal Nehru's *The Discovery of India*. Mum had an MA in Economics and History, was a lecturer for a few months before she married. She was leaving the south, for the first time. She was the first in the many generations of Naidus who was venturing to the North, a southern woman, alone, with its cold climates. She went in 1948 with their firstborn.

Emotional geographies and Multilingual Migrations 1948:

Gandhi was shot on January 31st. Shot dead, the father of the nation. Mother India was holding his heart in her open hand.

Mum is travelling with her firstborn, my brother. She is going from Madras Central Station near Moore Market, on a big steam engine rail train to cover some 2000 and more kilometres. She was with Yvonne Palmer, another officer's wife who had become a friend, also from the south. Both had a baby each, a year old – 'midnight's children'. They both spoke English and Tamil and crossing the Deccan had not realised how much the weather, the food, the language, the position of women would change on a train journey that took nearly fifty hours. They had left their mothers and their comfort zones with no guide books or maps, just their friendship spoken in English, and their laughter.

By the time September came, Mother was adjusting to Hindi and Punjabi and she was beginning to feel her English, reading and conversation, was not much use. It was the shopping for the shoes that made her flinch. She had not known what Delhi winter was. In Madras the well-known insider joke was: 'We have four seasons – hot, hotter, hottest, NE-Mon-sooooonh-like-the-South-China-Tai-phoon'. So, footwear was always, at least with Indians, open-toe and heel, slippers and sandals outdoors, and bare feet indoors. Mum had worn high-heeled sandals when visiting her brother as captain of his ship that had come to the port of Madras. But the prospect of wearing 'socks and shoes' was a shocker – "it's like going back to school!" she muttered about her memory of it. Worse still, of course, was the Delhi winter. Bone biting cold with a two-bar electric heater in the high-ceilinged rooms of a building known as King Edward's Mess.

Military cantonments are safe places, well-guarded except against drafts of cold winds. Some of the old colonial bungalows had coal fires but only in a single room, and my brother's tiny lungs caught a bronchial chill, flared into pneumonia and Mum was floundering with her new role as wife, mother, with an inconvenient language, and the wretched weather. The Gurkha ayah that she and Yvonne shared, discovered too late perhaps, had the best remedy according to her, to put children into a comfortable sleep; a dose of marijuana from the fingertip.

I remember my mother recounting this on a warm sultry afternoon with me under the ceiling fan of Chennai when we wished we could have a cold draft from Delhi.

Now it has so much meaning. When she recounted the story there was the recollection of a time and era when, as two young mothers, Yvonne and she could rescue their babies with vigour and learn a lesson from the chilblains of Delhi. They 'got on with it'. But she did say with her customary knitted brow at 70, "Oyo! I nearly lost my baby boy! It was like a monster. Biting, burning bone cold."

I could only think, "Mum, you were always a survivor! A champion!" The joke was always about eating Champion Oats, it makes you strong when washed down with Bournvita in the daytime and then Horlicks to keep warm at night.

It was the big migration from south and sea level to the red sand plains of the north. It wasn't about temperature or even food – Mother was adept in baking cakes and fluffy omelettes that astonished her English and Irish friends, as she was with the distinctive coconut milk crab curry, a specialty of the Naidu clan, as well as marinated Bombay duck eaten with tamarind rasam and rice that the departing British continued to call Mullagatawny; they fortunately were more discerning in not branding all Indian cuisine as 'curry' as they were sensitive enough to be aware curry constitutes a condiment of an entire process developed across twenty-five regions and their unique specialty cuisines. 'Curry' was adapted as populist, at times denigrating, parlance by a few Anglo-Indians and those back in England who presumed they knew what India was in a nutshell. What Jaya was getting us children to taste was the idea of 'mother-tongue'. Each condiment had its regional name – cinnamon (English), daalchinni (Hindi), Patte (Telegu/Tamil); pepper (E), kalimirch (H), mullaga (T/T); ginger (E), adhrak (H), injhiva (T/T). This is a slim example of daily parlance. It's not outdated. It was relevant then, and now as a celebration of multilingual India. Twenty-five literary languages, and 1500 dialects and assimilating English with regional nuances.

I'm indebted to the travel and grit my father's profession gave us. I'm grateful to my mother for integrating, with commentary and practice, the origins of her Telegu identity with her education in English in modernising Indians and having access to the world apart from the world wars. At a time when women were not considered a priority to be educated, here was Mother battling with the challenges of her own protective mother.

In later years, mother and I would compare our thoughts about belonging and separation in the epic *Ramayana* culminating in the celebration of the festival Deepavali for southerners, and Diwali for northerners, and the music systems and languages of the north, and the south of India.

Mothering, as I know it now, is turning a girl into a woman into a world of anxiety, with love. The willingness to leave family and love in another realm is unbearable, but it comes of itself to keep the life, of a life of one's own blood. I do not know of this for my own body.

It sticks in my stomach, my lungs, my throat. Not as a sickness, but as a very palpable part of my mother's transition from girl, woman, mother in an unsettled India, settling, alien in the north with the occasional southern mother tongue spoken between father and her in the evenings after formal social hours in English; a reminder the British left behind of monolingualism as constitutional neutrality and as a social norm.

Between north and south of work and life, marriage and my father's career, the children and the south, she always carried that stroke of luck, unconsciously working through her intuition, adept at carrying through her self-taught southern wisdom a way of softening the accents of all her northern counterparts.

It was the physical death of my mother that made me engage more with who my mother is and what mothering means. I became aware that she had seen my body bathed in blood arriving in the eighth month. I never saw her body be washed and dressed for the cremation. All she kept telling me in her last years was: 'The red sari for my cremation. I will be departing as a *su mangali*. A woman married, in marriage, not a widow."

After years and years of us being close friends as mother and daughter, sharing our humour and she my losses, it seemed strange that she was letting go of these appendages of children and was seeing herself as a woman, and then as a married one, leaving this world. We as children always think we come first.

Mothering: Earth

So it was Mother's Day. Now that my mother has been dead for 13 years, of course I don't send cards out to her, but I light a lamp in my imagination and in front of her photograph with that open smile showing her teeth. I used to send my husband's mother a card and flowers and speak on the phone. Now we are in a pandemic, and my husband's mother remembers the '40s well, as it was her childhood then, but not necessarily the clock time of our every day. My mother and my husband's mother are fifteen years apart, mine the older. Their love and friendship formed after their children met and they nurtured each other by a common language – English and 'Mothering'. It was about the experience of being mothers to similar children who had met across continents in the lit space of a theatre, strung with words creating new worlds of meaning. My husband

and I, each as children, and our mothers, were linked organisms across time, race, culture and faith and we endeavour to keep this chain of being together in spite of the 'missing', of me and my mother.

This year Mother's Day hit, hurt and it's a kind of healing, this hurting memory of 'missing' mother. Nothing unpleasant, just the ache that love brings. Of loss and a real unconditional love reawakened. It could well be because we are writing this Mothering epic – sometimes it feels like an elegy, and I hope it will be an *anagnorisis*...recognition of a time passed that brings new meaning of what was said and what flows into my life that I hold as precious. As precious as Unmai my Labrador's head deeply asleep on my foot and I don't want to wake her but just enjoy looking at that peaceful trusting, even greedy, sleep; I sacrifice not moving, as it would wake her.

It reminds me of my mother's tenderness and jolliness – planning for my time after her death. As if she would watch over me beyond her present body, she looked into the near distance. Her eyes soft and brown and moist as she looked into the unknown time ahead as we sat that afternoon after lunch and my father had gone for his siesta to his bed. We both were sitting side by side looking forward. We sat, her arm touching mine, like sisters in Amrita Shergill's paintings caught effortless in a wave of same-ness in our hearts, with the ceiling fan circling and slicing the air above us, in the moist humidity of May in Madras, as it was known then. She sighed. I felt a profound aphorism may appear. She turned her head and we looked at each other. She sighed and smiled. We were absolutely one at that moment. I knew she worried about my future, my dreams turning into hopes and awaiting news. I felt that ache in my spirit heart as if she had lit a flame there. Her smile was to say: "It's ok, I know you want to go. But..." and then her eyebrows wrinkled and her smile dropped as the tears flowed: "But, you must know how I feel. I feel they have taken my child away. You are always so far away..." and she swallowed and steadied herself. Her arm was still touching mine. *They* were the dreams to do the Ph.D., the words, to write. We were awaiting news about my admission to The University of Leeds.

"Ma! Please be happy for me!" I said.

"I am," she said, "But you must know how *your* mother *feels*."

I felt the strangest sensation of my heart being cleaved apart, and yet it was being filled with more love, and I cried. That is an experience of trans-mission. When a mother awakens in you what she 'contains' as Mother. She took her sari pallu from her left side that was closest to me and wiped my face as if I was a little girl.

"Know always that we have been together many lives before, I will always love you." She smiled that way that is of time and not of it. Indelible.

Yet, she had the capacity that mothers as chums do – flip the script from one scene to another.

"Let's have some of that walnut halwa I made!" she said.

Extraordinary cook that she was, I stuffed myself as getting emotional makes me ravenous. She kept chuckling as she spooned more halwa into my bowl.

She had a way of dragging the chair on the mosaic floor. Her hand was on its back, then she realised she would disturb Dad. Standing, with her plump and butter-soft hands on that wooden back of the chair she said: "Do you remember cows and calfs' party?" and we both started laughing. Guffawing, actually. In that heat, Dad awoke and came to the dining table and saw us streaming with tears of laughter. Turning to him she said "Come, have some tea. Now I can drag the chair without disturbing you!" Dad looked at me and winked.

"What's this about cows…?" Dad asks.

I'm scrolling dates back in my mind. From 1984 in Madras that afternoon, we are racing back in our minds to 1970. It's Washington DC. My father was having a momentary sulk. My stunning older sister, and I, were dressed and ready seventeen and thirteen years old repectively, in our saris. It was for The Cherry blossom parade on the Potomac. My sister bright and beautiful was selected to be on the United States President's yacht.

"So who all will be there?" Dad had asked.

"O we'll be mothers and daughters there." Mum was thirty years younger then and so radiant. Bursting out laughing she had said: "think of it as cows and their calves – each mother showing off her daughter!" We all laughed as my sister and I were explaining that being called a cow in England or the US had a whole unfashionable meaning – so beware!

Now, every time I return to Mammallapuram's coast where Mum selected a plot of land and she and Dad planted trees of tamarind, neem, coconut and mango for me, I walk to the cave sculptures. There, a sixth-century stone relief in the rock-cut cave is a cow, her tongue in mid-motion licking her calf. Even now, every tourist pats the granite cow and its calf. A wave of tenderness washes over local and tourist alike and a humanity of tenderness returns to us from a sculptor who carved the 'mother-ing' hundreds of years ago; remaining intimate yet anonymous.

This Mother's Day, my friend, sent me a film of a cow giving birth to a bull calf under her balcony on the banks of the Narmada river. All wet and out, the cow leaned her exhausted body over and found new vigour in licking the juices of life over and around her sleepy new calf.

It makes you weep that there is so much love, with and without words with animals, the earth, and mothers who let you go, and understand and are your friends, and tug you long after they are gone, and after three-score years, you are that idiot little girl nuzzling and hugging her when she comes home late at night after building the house we as a family spent such epic memories in.

It's 2020. The numbers look so slick together, ripe for a Tambola call out. Japan has redesigned the logo featuring 2 0 2 0, like numbers on the run – this is not just a year of elections, or the leap year. It is for many of us the year of the earth's adjustments.

Could Gaia's reasoning return to social conversations about how atmospheric carbon dioxide is kept in check? Carbon dioxide is pumped into the atmosphere by volcanoes, and removed by the weathering of rocks (encouraged by bacteria and plant roots in the soil). When it reaches the sea, the dissolved carbon dioxide is used by tiny organisms, known as coccolithophores (algae), to make their shells. When coccolithophores die they release a gas – dimethyl sulphate – which encourages the formation of clouds in the atmosphere. (The Guardian, 2016)

I'm thinking of a cow's tongue licking her calf; one organism of multiple organs feeding its own species and another. The cow's milk feeds humans. It's an emotive imprint we understand. I'm also beginning to understand how coccolithophores give us the atmosphere to breathe, the way earth knows what we're learning at great expense to learn about mothering.

Quiet force, daily activism

1969, Washington D.C.

This was a whole new world and when Jaya went for her voluntary work for three hours on alternate Fridays Downtown in the Hospital full of ambulances, sirens, addicts and old people who came for a cup of coffee and cookies they enjoyed the momentary suffering-free zone "with those kind ladies in Saris."

Mother was not an activist in the world of titles, but she was responsive and made things happen with sensitivity and a calm energy. She had exceptional communication abilities and valued life that she had known as precarious and easily lost, as she lost her father to Typhoid and Cholera within a matter of three days. She had seen her brother's wife Pramila so humbled by the destruction of the Pacific theatre of World War Two, of their family home in Burma, returning to Calcutta as a refugee, but her education made them kindred spirits in their reading, chanting of nursery rhymes, negotiating in the treatment of the cooks whom my grandmother had in her firing range of dismissals.

I remember vividly in Delhi in 1965 when she used to do voluntary work in the Military Hospital as a letter writer to the war wounded, she would also have to go to homes and read out the news of those killed in action. I used to accompany her, and not understanding what death meant, could see how she would sit, hold hands, and on leaving, follow up on a procedure for welfare and education for the deceased dependents left behind. As she had language skills in Tamil and Telegu, and was familiar with Gurkha regiments, she was asked to represent the Madras Regiment Welfare associations as well.

Then came the liberation of 'East Pakistan' to become Bangladesh. Father and Mother had regular sessions at home on McKinley Street, for interested friends and members of the community who wanted my father's expertise on the situation. Maps spread out, cups of tea, pecan cookies, semolina upumau on that polished, long mahogany table.

Then Raghu Rai's photographs of thousands of refugees coming in from Dhaka/East Bengal-Pakistan into Howrah/West Bengal – India living in circular cement pipes, men carrying their skeletal mothers, children malnourished, dogs and the maimed eating off the same scrap heap.

Mother mobilised a team for raising funds and food and blankets. She was elected Vice-President of CHETNA an Indian Women's organisation in Washington DC. This was voluntary and in collaboration with the inspirational President, Mekhala Jha. They got funds, medical supplies, food tins, fruits, water, airline couriers, and voluntary medical teams out to the sites. The awareness they created among local American communities, universities, schools, hospitals, churches, radio and TV, without a media officer, more for the humanitarian issue as Nixon and Kissinger were not India's allies. There's a wonderful photograph of Mamie Eisenhower and Mum. She's scribbled a note on the back about Bangladesh. I learned from Mother, that the real stress is after the wave of action is over. She knew how to keep her ego out, the strongest friendships in, and continue life with a philosophy of 'sensitivity as strength'. Old-fashioned, but wholesome. I was a teenager knowing with intense certainty that people like Mum never die. She gave me the freedom to pursue the Arts.

Mum was fifty-seven. In a world where that was considered old. She knew I was racing up to be her age, to be friends, and never let me know that age and ageing would tire me out with her increasing ill-health.

The Bindu. The Dot

2020
This is for her, Mother, and what she left behind.

1990:
It was as if her prayers were answered the day I announced I was to marry Chris. Not because I was getting married, but because the man himself is wise and kind beyond his years.

2003:
Then there was the book she left behind. *Soundarya Lahiri: Inundation of Divine Splendour* by Sri Sankaracharya who travelled from Kerala to Kashmir in the 9th Century.

05 July 2020
Guru Purnima – The Full moon celebrating gratitude to the Guru.

Jaya's wisdom about context, is a lesson I have not mastered. But I am sufficiently adept in understanding how this opened horizons to the secret of the inner life for her in enabling glimpses of that, in mine. She could take a profound philosophy and illustrate its genius in the daily rhythm of life, anywhere in the world, and with people from any culture, race, gender or faith. It is also possible she would not be able to hear the cynics. Her lack of hearing functioned as a filter, not to erode building bridges between people. While I will be recollecting how I understood the significance of the bindu, the dot, through her, I'm going to start with something that is happening here and now, in London and Costa Rica.

There are two verses from the Sanskrit that she gave me; in turn, I have given them to Veena's and Rupal's children, as well as four other children who make our group of seven children. The circle widens. This group was formed by a young friend, Mrinalini Ramakrishnan, in London. Her mother Arundhati Menon is someone who brought handloom saris back into design and fashion and is a close friend of my mother and my sister Viji. Arundhati suggested I tell stories from mythology to this group of children. Usha Aroor is a friend to all of us and opened my mind to the philosophical enquiry of the myths, along with my mother who gave me the Bhakti to understand the way the heart knows. For many years over quite a few years, the group between the ages of five to twelve, we recite the verses that were given to me by my mother and their grandparents, and indeed that signifies the bindu, the dot.

Both the verses celebrate the feminine force shakti; one as the concept of dynamic energy that we all interact in as a manifestation of *Devi*/feminine force, signified by the bindu, the dot. The other is the *Gayatri*, a call to pure consciousness beyond forms and names that is self-effulgent, light that is brighter than the sun, the gods, and represents the spirit of billions of universes pervading across time, removing layers of limitation that society imposes on us. When I put it across like this it sounds vast, vague and monstrously profound. But Jaya, my mother, had a way of living it through her life and left me a text called *Soundarya Lahiri* by Sankaracharya (800 BCE). It translates as the Praise song to the Shakti, Feminine Force or Tripurasundari (Three-point splendour). Mother was reading the text into her eighties before she died and making notes in English beside the Sanskrit and leaving marks for me about how these verses relate to the environment, evolution, consciousness and continuum.

Devi mantra:

> *Ya Devi sarva bhuteshu Maatri rupena samasthita*
> *namastasye namastasye namastasye namo namah.*(Sanskrit)

O Devi you pervade all that exists in your manifestation and essence as Mother, my salutations to you now and ever. (Tr. Mine.)

Gayatri mantra:

> *Om Bhur Bhuvah svah*
> *Tat Savitur Varenyam*
> *Bhargo Devasya Dhi Mahi*
> *dhi yo Yo na Prachodayat* (Sanskrit)

I salute that self-effulgent consciousness illumining the worlds, brighter than the sun, that it enlighten my being. (Tr. Mine)

These verses form the foundation of Indian systems of thought-experience-super consciousness or knowledge-existence-bliss. This 'experience' or realization permeates yoga, philosophy, Ayurveda, seasonal crops, staple, cuisine, ecology, literature, and the adventure to discover the Atman.

The bindu, or dot, functions as the mark that is the fixed point, but on floor patterns – kolam – between points are the movements, symbolising the systolic and diastolic rhythm, in circles, of the human being co-existing with all forms of life. The bindu, the dot on the forehead signifies the third eye, that experiences and projects the universe from within.

These concepts are embedded and woven and dyed in the very fabric of the stories and epics that I share with Veena's and Rupal's, and the other children as we look at fasts, feasts and the philosophy of festivals. My endeavour is to embrace their context, the natural world, and the creative force that is inspired by this… this bindu, the dot that enlarges from a fine still point to an ever-widening circle that encompasses all existence and knowledge.

While the seed of this way of looking and sharing with others had been planted in me a long while ago, I remember something vividly that sprouts the figure of bindu, the dot in a closer, intimate way I hold close about Mother passing a legacy on.

The bangle my mother gave me in 2006, was a braid of 24k. gold, naturally in a circle, and clasped with a round ruby dot. We were by Sukra Jewellers, by Mylapore Tank, Madras-Chennai, where dancers get their temple jewellery blessed by their gurus and at the shrine of the Kapileshwar temple dedicated to Nataraja the Shiva of Dance, for their debut *arangetram*. She said with her open smile as she held my right hand and closed it into a 'lotus bud form' and slipped the bangle through: "There! Now you know I'm always holding you by the hand!"

We went back home and she took it and placed it at the home shrine *puja* room. She then got Vanila the ayah to bring the ground rice powder to make a *kolam* floor pattern starting with three dots vertical north to south then horizontal east to west.

"Here's the *Bindu* the central dot, mentioned in the *Soundarya Lahiri*," and she added vertical and horizontal dots spaced at a hand-width. These were joined with rice powder flowing from her thumb and index finger creating a near-topographic map of a lotus. She placed the bangle, the strands of *malli* jasmine in the centre and instructed me to light the ghee in the brass lamp with five wicks. All of which I did, because this is what daughters do when a mother in the south silently transmits something through the matriarchal line; followed by listening to devotional music. Eleven years later, Caryn brought me bangles from South Africa and slipped them onto my wrist. Finely braided copper with silver dots marking distances, shining like tiny suns, bringing hearts and worlds closer.

I've always been mesmerised by spheres. In drawing, when you watch artists being trained in India, Ganesha is often started with circles, and then triangles. This is pure geometry and mathematics of Islam and Hindu worlds that create points of resilient strength in buildings too. The sphere of the bangle is not an emptiness, it encircles a source of energy, the wrist that joins the hand to the arm and so on. In building houses, which my mother did for all of us, she would stand in the heat under the sphere of an umbrella and watch the architect draw angles and elevation, starting from a dot and joining the multiple dots with a string.

The dot, or bindu, on the forehead that women particularly wear, signi-fied the third eye, the centre of illumination, the focus that wards off the 'evil eye', more than solely symbolising marriage, or womanhood. The dot began in red, or black, or white, and from it there were variations that swirled into fashion statements in my youth.

My mother belonged to music choirs and sang at festivals in her later years as well, and these were particularly to do with the praise song to Devi – a consort, a warrior, the resplendent, the super-sensuous dancer, the goddess of identity through language and speech, with her staff of sugarcane the crop that nourished and built shelter, the rosary of constant remembrance that the visible is ephemeral and the invisible the discovery; the empty alms bowl to be filled in all seasons of drought and cornucopia.

So, when she gave me the *Devi* mantra, she mentioned: "mothering is about *knowi*ng when the right time is." So, when people whom I had never met in my life before brought their children, it happened to be the right time, of a spiritual DNA, that will or will not work through the children's memory, of passing on the mantra of the Bindu, the dot, of connectivity, whatever their ages, their future – we have a momentum of our Bindu, dot across our human line.

I had wanted to write something factual and substantial about Mother and cannot. Her sister-in-law from Burma, Pramila was her good friend. And they both used to talk when I was a child about the novels they read while my Radiant Reader for KinderGarten was spread on the lap of my aunt, while my head slept on my mother's lap. I felt I had two mothers in the evenings and none during the day. Mother was away building the house and my aunt was on housekeeping duty by the time I came home from school. Excess and abstinence were always the see-saw that I played with in my life; it began an early desire to find the company of the tama-rind tree by the well and start telling stories to my right and left hands – we were the three points of a triangular companionship.

I saw my mother in 2005 for my parents' 60th wedding anniversary. She was frail by then. When I hugged her before leaving for the airport, I knew it would be the last time I could hold her like this, and she held on to me; I was mothering Mother. We both knew this current of strong love had been, as we believed, in many lifetimes before. For a Hindu woman, particularly until mother's generation, whatever impact history, education, society, modernisation may have made, the dot was the symbol of completeness and auspiciousness. For all rites, housewarming, childbirth, marriages of children, festivals, the Devi of the household is present to make the rituals whole.

When I kept returning to England with a heavy heart, she would call and say: "Remember the red sari." It was of course to be the one she wanted to be dressed in for the cremation. I was to meet her and with my father and brother and his family; we would all be going to Delhi for my sister's son's wedding. Mother died three days before that. I could not make it for her cremation.

It is what happens with distances and what makes for diaspora like me; the time is never and always, right. Like her, I'm learning not to hold on to what is not in my control. I hold on to the dot of concentration, and the ever-widening circle of its power, of love. In more ways than one, I have grieved for her since 2007, when I turned into a new decade the bangle she gave me was to enter this phase.

In 2012, I was fascinated by posters of the Yayoi Kusama's posters all over the London underground advertising her exhibition at TATE Modern. I remember crying through all the rooms as the dot kept dancing in multiples off the wall, the canvas, the installations. I cried and cried alone feeling like the boy in Akira Kurosawa's film *Dreams* about the Kitsune – the foxes' wedding – allured away yet alienated from 'home'. With relief, with understanding, with loss, with completion of knowing the right moment. Of realising liberation is about being an orphan in constant movement meeting others moving toward the hope of freedom and the unknown ahead, and knowing the strength of a love, in my case real, and fulfilled.

Smt. Jayarukmini Naidu, MA
1924-2007
Madras-Chennai

Kusama was born five years after my mother, and they would have shared a similar upbringing balancing tradition and national policy during World War Two. For me, they made the bridge between east and east with the dot, the sun. This is what Yayoi talks about when in the '50s she creates her artistic signature of the polka dot.

For Yayoi Kusama the dot:

…has the form of the sun, which is a symbol of the energy of the whole world and our living life, and also the form of the moon, which is calm-round, soft colourful senseless and unknowing. Polka dots can't stay alone; like the communicative life of people, two or three polka-dots become movement. Polka dots are a way to infinity…we become part of the unity of our environment.

I have nothing more to say. So, I'll end with my poem that is as much about birth and death and life; connecting dots coming full circle.

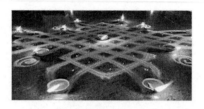

Abhishekham

Water falls
Milk pours
Turmeric balms the black stone deity.
Saree weaves
Jasmines cluster
Diamonds wink
Flames dilate as
Oil wells from the brass lamp with five mouths.
Coins flick between nimble fingers of the six a.m. temple priest on duty.
Mother sits hands clasped facing the goddess.
As temple bells toll overhead
Her prayers heighten:
"For this girl, give her hope, husband and fertility."
These words have passed her lips earlier.
This time after that prodigal return:
"Where her eye is battered, o goddess of all rivers, balm it with sight.
Let there be peace with love."
Slow dissolve, our furrows deepen.
I see the last vestige of unconditional love flow
Into the pool of milk and turmeric, jasmine, oil and ash
Rushing in the gutter by the feet of the goddess.
The song to river Ganga
Finds a new meaning in Mother.
My birthday passes.

ABOUT THE AUTHORS

Cathy Hull began her career as a community tutor forty years ago establishing an adult education centre based in a comprehensive school. She has held senior posts in education including at Goldsmith's University and the University of Kent. A focus of her work has been helping adults to value their informal experiential learning. At Macmillan, she established Macmillan Open Learning with programmes validated by over twenty-five UK universities and 22,000 students globally. Cathy has taught comparative literature for over forty years which together with her passion for memoirs has inspired this reflection on her mother.

Kumi Konno was born in Tokyo, Japan, in 1959. She studied at Chelsea College of Arts in London. Her writing includes several series of articles for Japanese design magazines and a translation of an interior design book. She has curated national and international exhibitions of contemporary art and craft. She has always been interested in the methodology of creation; the relationship between human memory and creativity. This is her first foray into memoir writing.

Dr Vayu Naidu-Banfield: Inspired by her mother Jayarukmini Naidu MA, Vayu's PhD in Leeds on Epic Storytelling led to projects in HM Prisons – reflecting on the positive impact of stories on diverse inmates; in Battered Women's Shelters as myths of Mother as woman. Vayu Naidu Storytelling Theatre created intercultural performance productions touring internationally and Britain. During her AHRC Post-doctoral research on migration, mental health, multilingual literacy, she met Cathy Hull in Canterbury who mentored Learning for Lecturers. With Dr Caryn Solomon, she co-created storytelling awakening the human in organizational development. Novels: 'Sita's Ascent'; 'The Sari of Surya Vilas'; www.vayunaidu.com

Dr Rupal Shah has been a GP in the same Inner London practice for the past seventeen years. She has been immersed in her patients' stories over this period and has come to realise that stories and health are inextricably intertwined; so that now, writing her own feels like a natural progression. Rupal has a background in medical writing and also works as an Associate Dean for Health Education England, with a particular focus on promoting inclusion in training and reducing bias. She is married to Alistair and has two daughters, Anya and Ava.

Veena Siddharth is a human rights advocate. She has worked on poverty, women's rights, reproductive rights, and exclusion in Asia, Africa and Latin America. In writing her mother Saroja's story, Veena aims to examine how we create new roots and connections when we leave what is familiar. Veena speaks several languages including Spanish, Nepali, Tamil, Italian and French. She finds inspiration in playing the viola in a chamber group and frequent walks in nature. Veena lives in Costa Rica with her husband Seth, son Kailash and daughter Leela.

Dr Caryn Solomon: Caryn began her career teaching Social Psychology and the Psychology of Women at Boston University. Forty years later, she ended it teaching Organisation Development at the London School of Economics. In between, she headed up an Organisation Development team in an international company for fifteen years and was a consultant to many organisations in different parts of the world. What she has learned throughout is the power of narrative – the transformative impact of stories in both the telling and the hearing. Storytelling has been a feature of Caryn's family. This story is one her mother helped to tell.